I0211998

PAUL'S LETTER —TO— LEADERS

PHILIPPIANS FOR ELDERS AND DEACONS

Dr. James Estep

Paul's Letter to Leaders
Philippians for Elders and Deacons

Copyright © 2025 College Press Publishing
www.Collegepress.com

Cover Design by College Press

Unless otherwise indicated, all Scripture quotations are from The ESV® Bible (The Holy Bible, English Standard Version®), © 2001 by Crossway, a publishing ministry of Good News Publishers. Used by permission. All rights reserved.

Scripture quotations marked (NIV) are taken from the Holy Bible, New International Version®, NIV®. Copyright © 1973, 1978, 1984, 2011 by Biblica, Inc.™ Used by permission of Zondervan. All rights reserved worldwide. www.zondervan.com. The "NIV" and "New International Version" are trademarks registered in the United States Patent and Trademark Office by Biblica, Inc.™

ISBN 978-0-89900-133-3 (Paperback)
ISBN 978-0-89900-137-1 (Hardback)
ISBN 978-0-89900-150-0 (E-book)

Dedication

To Wally and Barbara Rendel

For your faithfulness to Christ, example of His Love, commitment to sharing His Gospel in word and deed, advancing the Kingdom, and loyal ministry spanning over six decades.

I cannot even begin to itemize, estimate, or express the influence you have had on my life, faith, family, and ministry.

Love & Thank You Both!

Table of Contents

Introduction

Why *Philippians* for leaders? Why not another one of Paul's letters? Philippians is unique in that it was written not only to the disciples in Philippi, but specifically to the "overseers and deacons" (1:1). This has been recognized as part of the letter's uniqueness for centuries. Chrysostom (4th century A.D.) wrote, "Nowhere else does Paul write specifically to the clergy – not in Rome, in Corinth, in Ephesus, or anywhere. Rather, he typically writes jointly to all who are holy, faithful and beloved. But in this case, he addresses specifically the bishops and deacons. Why? Because it was they who had borne fruit and they who had sent Epaphroditus to him."[1]

This prompts the question, "What does Paul say to leaders, both then and now?" This study of Philippians will focus on three necessary questions:

- What did Paul say to the Philippian believers? (general message)

- What did Paul imply to the church's leaders? (specific message)

- What does Paul say to us today about leading His people? (current application)

Essentially, what did Paul say to the Philippian overseers and deacons, and how does his message inform our ministry *today*? What principles for today's leaders are present in Paul's letter to the Philippian congregation with its leaders?

As a cofounder of e2: effective elders (e2elders.org) I have had my share of engagements, conversations, equipping seminars, and prayers with church leaders. I am acutely aware of the needs of today's congregations and their leaders. Reading Philippians, the message to contemporary church leaders sounds more and more familiar, specifically to those who are serving as overseers/elders and deacons.

About this Book

Allow me to be candid. I lack the creativity of Calvin Miller's *The Philippian Fragment* (IVP, 1982), a whimsical but insightful novel based on a fabricated archaeological find of a second century manuscript regarding the interactions of the Philippian congregation. This study is *not* intended to be an academic paper or commentary, but one that extracts the principles of leadership from the instructions of Paul to the Philippian overseers and deacons, the leaders of the church. However, I utilized a variety of commentaries in exploring the biblical text to expose the most significant insights for church leaders. Figure 1.1 contains a list of the commentaries that I consulted, ranging from those that were more practical in content, focusing on application of the biblical text, to those more academic in their approach, such as assuming a knowledge of biblical Greek, theological matters, or historical backgrounds.

This study is not a traditional commentary, rather it is a study of Philippians from the perspective of leaders in the church, overseers/ elders and deacons. Throughout the letter, Paul addresses not only the congregation, but specifically its leadership. However, he also does not hesitate to identify opposition, both from inside the church and from outside the church. This study will treat each section of Philippians in five parts:

- **THE TEXT** Unless otherwise indicated, the Bible text is from the English Standard Version (ESV). Selected Greek terms that require special attention, will be transliterated in brackets within the ESV text.
- **TEXT QUESTIONS** A set of content and open-ended questions based on the specific passage of Philippians to prime the proverbial pump for study and later discussions.[2]
- **INTO THE TEXT** A general commentary on the text of Philippians, highlighting Paul's message to leaders and their opponents. It will not take the form of the traditional, academic commentary that moves verse-by-verse.
- **INSIGHTS FROM THE TEXT** This section itemizes the leadership lessons, the take-aways, from Paul's letter to the

Philippian leaders, with additional information and insight for today's overseers-elders and deacons.
- **PERSONAL AND TEAM REFLECTION** A series of open-ended questions or learning exercises facilitates application of each chapter. These are designed to aid in making practical, tangible use of reading the text.

How to Use this Book

As with any book, it can be used for personal edification and equipping. An individual leader could choose to devote time to personal, solo study of the book. In fact, a leadership team could also choose to study the book, each on their own. However, a second way to make use of the text would be to have the leadership team jointly read the text for not only personal instruction, but to facilitate a joint learning experience. To do this, dedicate a portion of the leadership meeting to a chapter of the book, answer the reflection questions together; or use the entire book at a leadership retreat. A third possible use of the book could be for potential leaders, those not yet in leadership but who are considering it. The book could be part of the process of vetting potential leaders, or it could be part of onboarding for new leaders. Perhaps a mentor, a leader who has already read through the text, could guide and discuss the book with the potential leader(s). In any case, the ultimate intended use of the book is to equip leaders to minister more effectively.

A Final Note

Another reason I selected Philippians, is that the church at Philippi continued to attract and intrigue church leaders for decades after Paul's ministry was concluded. Two apostolic fathers, church leaders who served in the century following the apostles, continued to write to the Philippian church with great admiration. Likewise, later church authorities wrote letters to the Philippian congregation offering affirmation and gentle correction, just as Paul had done in his letter. Paul's letter to the Philippians continued to receive ample attention from the early church with notable men writing sermons, homilies, and commentaries on the text. Men such as Chrysostom,

Augustine, Theodoret, Ambrosiaster, and others appealed to Philippians for wisdom and guidance . . . just as we do today. My hope is that, just as their study of Philippians gave them insight to serve and lead, centuries after it was written, it will speak to us as the 21st century church.

I started writing this book in Lincoln, Illinois while teaching at Lincoln Christian University, but finished it at my current ministry, Dallas Theological Seminary. Much of the writing and editing was completed on the Amtrak's Texas Eagle between the two.

Please know that I will be praying for all of you who are using this book as a means to motivate your ministry, fortify your faith in Jesus Christ, and direct your service as leaders in the church and wherever God has planted you.

Lead Well!

James Riley Estep, Jr., D.Min., Ph.D.
Dallas, Texas
A.D. 2025

Commentaries on Philippians

Practical

Sandra Glahn, *Frappe with Philippians* (Hillsboro, OR: AMG Publishers, 2009).

William Barclay, *Daily Study Bible: The Letters to the Philippians, Colossians, and Thessalonians* (Louisville: Westminster John Knox Press, 1975).

Frank Thielman, *The NIV Application Commentary: Philippians* (Grand Rapids: Zondervan Publishing, 1995).

Tony Merida and Francis Chan, *Christ-Centered Exposition: Exalting Jesus in Philippians* (Nashville: Holman Reference, 2016).

Lynn H. Cohick, *The Story of God Bible Commentary: Philippians* (Grand Rapids: Zondervan, 2013).

F.F. Bruce, *Understanding the Bible Commentary Series: Philippians* (Grand Rapids: Baker Book House, 1989).

Ralph P. Martin, *The New Century Bible Commentary: Philippians* (Grand Rapids: Eerdmans Publishing, 1980)

J.A. Motyer, *The Bible Speaks Today: The Message of Philippians* (Downers Grove, IL: InterVarsity Press, 1984).

N.T. Wright, *Philippians* (Downers Grove, IL: InterVarsity Press, 2009).

Gordon D. Fee, *IVP New Testament Commentary, Philippians* (Downers Grove, IL: InterVarsity Press, 1999).

Academic

F.F. Bruce, *New International Biblical Commentary: Philippians* (Peabody, MA: Hendrickson Publishers, 1989).

Jac J. Müller, *The New International Commentary on the New Testament: The Epistle of Paul to the Philippians and Philemon* (Grand Rapids: Eerdmans, 1983).

Richard R. Melick, Jr. *The New American Commentary: Philippians, Colossians, Philemon* (Nashville: Broadman Press, 1991).

James W. Thompson and Bruce W. Longenecker, *Paideia Commentaries on the New Testament: Philippians and Philemon* (Grand Rapids: Baker Academic Publisher, 2019).

Moisés Silva, *Baker Exegetical Commentary on the New Testament: Philippians, 2nd Edition* (Grand Rapids: Baker Academic, 2005).

Gordon D. Fee, *New International Commentary on the New Testament: Paul's Letter to the Philippians* (Grand Rapids: Eerdmans, 2015).

George Hunsinger, *Brazos Theological Commentary on the Bible: Philippians* (Grand Rapids: Brazos Press, 2020).

Mark J. Edwards ed., *Ancient Christian Commentary on the Scripture: New Testament VIII – Galatians, Ephesians, Philippians* (Downers Grove, IL: InterVarsity Press, 2005).

Joseph H. Hellerman, *Philippians, Exegetical Guide to the Greek New Testament* (Nashville: Broadman and Holman, 2015).

Thomas Moore, *Big Greek Idea Series: An Exegetical Guide for Preaching and Teaching – Philippians* (Grand Rapids: Kregel Academic, 2019).

Marvin R. Vincent, *Critical and Exegetical Commentary on the Epistles to the Philippians and to Philemon* (Edinburgh: T & T Clark, 1976).

Mark J. Keown, *Evangelical Exegetical Commentary, Philippians, 2 Volumes, 1:1-2:18; 2:19-4:23* (Bellingham, WA: Lexham Press, 2017).

Hermann L. Strack und Paul Billerbeck, *Kommentar Zum Neuen Testament Aus Talmud und Midrasch* (Munchen: C. H. Beck'sche Verlangsbuchhandlung, 1969).

Commentaries on Philippians

Chapter 1

Paul, the Philippians, and the "Overseers and Deacons" (1:1-2)

Why Philippians for leaders? Why not 1 and 2 Timothy, or Titus, or any other part of the New Testament? Philippians is unique in that it is written not only to the disciples in Philippi, but specifically to their "overseers and deacons" (1:1). Paul singled them out as a readily recognized group in the church at Philippi. As with his other letters, his letter to the Philippian church was meant to be received and read aloud during a church gathering, such as a worship assembly (see Col. 4:16, 1 Thes. 5:27). The Philippian believers recognize the carrier of the letter, presumably Epaphroditus (2:25, 4:18), and after their greeting, he holds up a letter from Paul. As the congregation is assembled, the letter is read. It opens, "Paul and Timothy, servants of Christ Jesus, To all the saints in Christ Jesus who are at Philippi, with the overseers and deacons . . ." (1:1). Can you imagine how the church leaders reacted when hearing it read for the first time? "Paul's writing to us!" Not to mention the reaction of the congregation when hearing the phrase "overseers and deacons," the slight glances, stares given to them, or raised eyebrows.

Have you ever seen a meercat quickly popping its head out of the desert ground, often with a look of shock or alertness on its face ? I can only image that the overseers and deacons, who were excited to hear what Paul had to share, now gave special attention to the letter. Is Paul disappointed in us? Is he pleased? *What was it saying to them, both as believers, and as leaders among the saints in Philippi?*

THE TEXT

Philippians 1:1-2 1 Paul and Timothy, servants [*douloi*] of Christ Jesus, To all the saints [*hagiois*] in Christ Jesus who are at Philippi, with the overseers [*episkopois*] and deacons [*diakonois*]: 2 Grace [*charis*] to you and peace [*eirēnē*] from God our Father and the Lord Jesus Christ.

TEXT QUESTIONS

- How does Paul's identification as a servant of Christ in Philippians 1:1 shape our understanding of leadership and authority in the Christian Community?
- Who are the letter's two authors/senders mentioned in Philippians 1:1?
- In what ways does the inclusion of both Paul and Timothy as authors of the letter influence the message and tone of Philippians 1:1-2?
- To whom is the letter addressed in Philippians 1:1?
- Why do you think they specifically mentioned "overseers and deacons"?

INTO THE TEXT

Who is sending the letter? Who wrote it? While the letter opens with the reference to both Paul and Timothy as the senders, the letter is undeniably written by Paul since the writer begins using first person, "I", immediately after the salutation (1:3-26), and later, the writer refers to Timothy in the third person (2:19-23), so while it may have had two senders, it had only one writer, Paul. What is interesting about the salutation in Philippians is that Paul doesn't refer to himself as an apostle, as he does in the majority of his letters, but only as a "servant," literally slave (*doulos*). Many modern English translations translate *doulos* as *servant* or *bond-servant* simply because these terms accurately reflect one who submits to servitude, as opposed to slaves who were *not* in servitude voluntarily. Elsewhere, Paul refers to himself as Apostle (Rom. 1:1; 1 Cor. 1:1; 2 Cor. 1:1; Gal. 1:1;

Eph. 1:1; 1 Tim. 1:1; 2 Tim. 1:1; Titus 1:1), but Philippians opens more like Thessalonians (1 Thes. 1:1; 2 Thes. 1:1; Phlm. 1). Only the Thessalonian correspondences have a similar personal introduction, but 1 and 2 Thessalonians lack the reference to church leaders. This makes Philippians the most unique salutation of any of Paul's letters! This curious absence of *apostle* is probably due to his familiarity with the congregation. The early church father Ambrosiaster (4th century A.D.) said: "He [Paul] keeps silent about his status as an apostle. He is writing to people who already know who he is and have an informed opinion of him."[3]

Why did Paul write this letter?

To put it simply, he couldn't visit them for a third time due to his incarceration. Philippians is part of what have been deemed the "Prison Epistles;"[4] Paul referring to his "imprisonment" (1:13, 17). One question is, "From where is he writing?" A variety of local authorities frequently incarcerated Paul: Ephesus, Caesarea Maritime, Rome. *Why do we assume it was Rome?* Four basic reasons favor Rome as his current incarceration: (1) Paul mentions being in the vicinity of the "imperial guard," or "palace guard" (NIV). The actual Greek term is *praitōriō*, Caesar's personal *Praetorian* guard (1:13). (2) Paul sends greetings from those of "Caesar's household" (4:22). (3) His situation (1:13, 4:22) seems to fit the description of his imprisonment in Rome at the close of Acts 28, c. A.D. 60, and not his later, more restrictive, Roman imprisonment depicted in 2 Timothy, specifically 4:16-17. Finally, (4) church tradition, dating to the early 2nd century, favors Rome as the site of his imprisonment. Hence, Rome seems to be the most favorable option.

Philippians is often regarded as a friendship letter. This is reflected in the informal greeting previously mentioned as well as the frequent use of "joy", occurring five times (1:4, 25; 2:2, 29; 4:1) and "rejoice" eleven times (1:18; 2:17, 18, 28; 3:1; 4:4, 10). Paul writes this letter to encourage believers, encouragement beyond their current circumstances. It is not a matter of joy due to material gain, political success, or the mere absence of opposition, but the personal hope of eternity and unity in the Christian community through faith in Jesus Christ. In Philippians, Paul frequently sets our current earthly life juxtaposed to our spiritual life in Christ now and in eternity (1:6, 21; 2:12-13; 3:10-14, 20; 4:6-7, 13, 19). This is indeed written by a friend to friends for friends.

However, opposition to Paul is present in Philippi. The church at Philippi may seem ideal but it was not perfect. A careful reading of the text shows Paul's indication of opposition. For example, "*Some* indeed preach Christ from envy and rivalry, but *others* from good will" (Phil. 1:5). "Because of my chains, *most* of the brothers in the Lord have been encouraged to speak the word of God more courageously and fearlessly" (Phil. 1:14). In fact, the unique introduction to the letter, the way in which Paul includes the congregation's leaders, possibly indicates that "tensions surrounded leaders and perhaps their supporters."[5] Not everyone at Philippi was prone to support Paul, some were opportunistic in his absence, and others opposed him openly. Either way, Paul had opposition at Philippi!

Some commentators say the opposition that the disciples faced at Philippi was from Jewish dissenters, Judaizers, and/or Romans loyal to the emperor and his cult. However, the opposition here is not persecution from without, but conflict from *within* the Philippian congregation. The opposition seems to be between two groups, and influences key leadership factors in Philippi, as noted in Figure 1.1.

It is essentially Paul, the Philippian leaders, and most of the congregation in opposition to those who were self-driven opportunists and those who disagreed with Paul's leadership. As we study the text, these points of opposition will be addressed as they occur in the text.

	Motives	
	Purposes	
	Character	
Paul, Leaders, &	*Commitments*	Opponents &
Congregation	*Integrity*	Opportunists
	Values	
	Effect on the	
	Church	

Figure 1.1

To Whom did Paul Write the Letter?

The salutation says to all the saints, *hagios*, the "holy ones," in Philippi. It is penned to the entire congregation, not just a select set or group as indicated in 1:1, but also 3:1; 4:1, 15). *Hagios* is a general term of identity and description for Christians. Paul persecuted the *hagios* before he was one himself (Acts 9:13) and Peter used the term to describe the believers in Lydda (Acts 9:32). Written to the entire congregation – "all the saints," 1:1, but also 3:1 and 4:1, 15. However, the word *saints* has led to the misnomers of a distinctive group within the church who possess a higher level of piety or righteousness than other believers. *No*, the term is applied to all of those in the church at Philippi, and to all of us reading the letter today. The term is a call for believers to live a distinctive life, different from those around them.

What is that distinctive? Without belaboring the point, the next phrase explains it: "in Christ Jesus." The Philippian *saints* are those who are "in Christ Jesus." Later in Philippians, he would use this "in Christ Jesus" inclusiveness to indicate all the Christians (4:20-21). The phrase is so significant in defining what it means to be a disciple, Paul uses the phrase "in Christ Jesus" a total of 51 times in his writings. Additionally, parallel phrases, such as "in Christ" occur 37 times, "in Jesus Christ" 3 times, and "in Jesus" twice.[6] Simply put, those who are in Christ Jesus are made righteous by his work on the cross (Rom. 3:23, 5:18, 6:23). It is not by our own merit or works (Eph. 4:1-10), which lends itself to the notion of a saint-class of Christians, but as Christians we are all in Christ, we are all saints. In a word: Grace!

What Do We Know About Philippi?

Paul's letter is written to a church that exists with a backdrop of Roman culture, society, religion, philosophy, and leadership. What kind of city was Philippi?

Historic: When we hear the name, Gettysburg, we don't think of the small town in southeastern Pennsylvania with a population of less than 8,000. We remember it as the Civil War's decisive battle in 1863. When Romans heard the name Philippi, they remembered the decisive Battle of Philippi in 42 B.C. that ended the Roman civil war following the assassination of Julius Caesar. Philippi was originally a small village named Krenides, but Phillip II, King of Macedonia, changed it to Philippi in 356 B.C. Following the Battle of Philippi, it was no longer considered a small Macedonian city but a growing Roman colony (Figure 1.2).

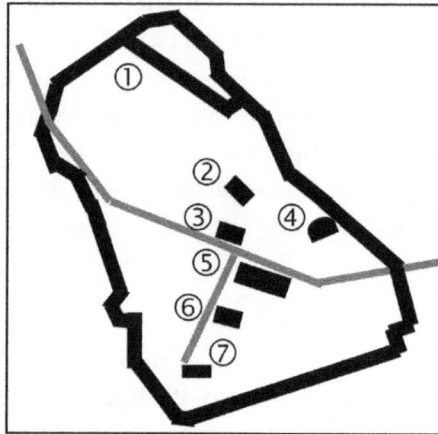

① Acropolis ② Egyptian Temple
③ Prison ④ Theater ⑤ Forum
⑥ Marketplace/Agora ⑦ Baths

Figure 1.2

Roman: While it may have started with a Greek culture, as a Roman colony its population was treated as citizens of Italy, with local government, free of taxes and imperial fees, and the rule of Roman law. This is probably why Luke describes Philippi as "a Roman colony" (Acts 16:12), while not designating other cities as such (for example, Antioch of Pisidia, Iconium, and Lystra).[7] In fact, as one approaches the city, the road signs and mile markers were written in Latin.[8] Veterans of the Roman legions were attracted to Philippi with its colonial designation and affirmation of Roman benefits. Remember, a *Roman* jailer was one of Paul's converts.

Influential: Luke describes Philippi as a *prōtē* city, translated *chief* or *first* (Acts 16:12). However, Thessalonica was the provincial capital, and Amphipolis was the district or county seat, so Philippi could not be considered a capital. What did Luke mean by *prōtē*? Simply put, Philippi was an influential city in the area. Because the city was located near both gold and silver mines, it was an economic hub in the region. This would fit Paul's pattern of strategically selecting cities from which the gospel could be carried further.

Waypoint: The old phrase "All roads lead to Rome!" is true of Philippi. The *Via Egnatia*, the primary Roman road extending from Rome through its western provinces, went through Philippi, bringing commerce, culture, information, and a steady flow of visitors (see Figure 1.3). This may have added to its influence as a leading city. Paul himself would have most probably used the *Via Egnatia* as he entered the city.

Figure 1.3

Urban Culture: Philippi was not a village or town, it was a city, with all the cultural centers that typify a Greco-Roman city. Figure 1.3 illustrates the city of Philippi, containing an acropolis, amphitheater, agora (market), hot spring baths, a city forum, and a variety of temples (Greek, Roman, and even Egyptian). It was indeed a cultured city, one resembling Rome more than Greece or Macedonia. Economically, Philippi was a production center, rather than an agricultural one. Remember, Lydia, the first European convert to Christ, was a seller of purple linen.

Religious: All of the above cultural factors led to a diverse religious setting, ranging from local cults to Greek and Roman deities, including an imperial cult, and even international eastern religions. Given the Roman population, obviously the imperial cult of Caesar was dominant, with a plethora of priests/priestesses, shrines and temples dedicated to the emperor. In spite of its dominance, Philippi likewise had worship sites for other deities, particularly from the eastern provinces, such as Asia Minor, Syria, and Egypt. Don't forget, one of Paul's converts was a demon-possessed slave girl! However, Philippi apparently did not have a Jewish presence. Luke does not mention a synagogue nor any engagement with a Jewish community, and no archaeological evidence or inscriptions exists to support a Jewish presence in Philippi. In fact, Acts 16:13 says, "on the Sabbath day we went outside the gate to the riverside, where we *supposed* there was a place of prayer . . ." but found a gathering of women, not a synagogue.

What Do We Know About the Philippian Church?

Fortunately, not only does the letter itself have several insights into the church itself, but we also have Luke's record in Acts of Paul's second missionary journey on which the church of Philippi was planted. N.T. Wright observes about the Philippian church's founding:

> For Paul, bringing the gospel to Greece (described in Acts 16:9-12) was like a completely new beginning (see Philippians 4:15). Although he had been preaching and planting churches in Asia Minor (modern Turkey) for some while, he seems to have had a sense that when he came into Europe he really was in new territory, and that if the gospel took root here it would prove in a further sense just how powerful it was. These, after all, were the Macedonians and Greeks, who had given the world one of its greatest cultures to date! And the Philippian church was the first of those churches on Greek soil.[9]

Let's look at the sequence of events in the life of the Philippian church from its inception to Paul's writing his letter to them.

- Paul receives the vision calling him to Macedonia (Acts 16:9-11).

- The congregation is planted by Paul on the 2nd Missionary Journey, along with Silas and Luke (Acts 16:12-40, c. AD 48-51).

   Note: Three Philippian conversion accounts are given in Acts 16: Lydia (16:11-15), demon-possessed slave girl (16:16-24), and a Roman jailer (16:25-34).

- Paul briefly visits the Philippian church on the 3rd Missionary Journey (Acts 20:6)

- The Philippians learn of Paul's imprisonment in Rome, they send Epaphroditus to aid him.

- Oppression and opposition to Paul *rises*, and continues (cf. 1 Thes. 2:2, "we had already suffered and been shamefully treated at Philippi").

- Epaphroditus arrives in Rome with a gift from the Philippians for Paul.

- Epaphroditus falls ill, Paul acknowledges their gift (4:18, 2:26).

- Paul receives word from Philippi of their distress over Epaphroditus (2:26).

- Paul writes the letter to the Philippian church.

- Epaphroditus takes Paul's letter to Philippi (2:25, c. A.D. 60).

- Timothy is soon to visit Philippi and is to report back to Paul (2:19).

Paul's letter to the Philippian church was one point of contact he had with them, but not the only one. He had planted the congregation, returned to it, received assistance from it while in his house arrest in Rome, and now writes them a letter to them in his absence.

21

"With Overseers and Deacons"

Unlike any other letter Paul penned, in addition to the greeting "to all the saints," the entire congregation, it includes the congregation's overseers (*episkopos*) and deacons (*diakonos*). Paul addresses the overseers, not elders (*presbeuteros*) or shepherds (*poimen*); although the three terms describe the same function, role, or position in the church (cf. Acts 20:17, 28; Titus 1:5, 7; 1 Tim 3:1-2; 1 Peter 5:1, 5; cf. 1 Pet. 2:25 where it is used of Christ in relation to his role as Shepherd). The term *episkopos* denotes a function or role, as reflected in the translation "overseer," and not as some translations favor *bishops*, emphasizing the position or title (KJV, RSV, and NEB). It should be noted that Paul refers to a plurality of overseers; consistent with elsewhere throughout the New Testament, elders and deacons are plural (Acts 14:23; 20:17, 28; 1 Tim. 3:1-7, 5:17-19; Titus 1:5-7; James 5:14; 1 Pet. 4:1-2). Paul refers to the "council of elders" (1 Tim. 4:14).[10]

Paul describes the "leaders" of the church in Thessalonica as "honor those who are your leaders in the Lord's work. They work hard among you and give you spiritual guidance" (1 Thes. 5:12). Now, Paul uses a term *episkopoi*, which we translate "overseers," but could readily mean "those who exercise oversight," like in Acts 20:28.

The overseers in the Philippian population lead alongside deacons. The term *deacon* is a transliteration of the Greek *diakonos*. Paul mentions deacons in 1 Timothy 3:8-13, written in A.D. 68, some eight years after Philippians. This makes Philippians 1:1 the earliest reference to deacons by name in the New Testament. Many scholars identify the Seven appointed by the Apostles in Acts 6:1-7 as deacons, primarily because the term *diakonia*, the verb form of *diakonos*, is used in Acts 6:1, translated *distribution*, and 6:4, translated *ministry*.[11] If this is the case, we have a very early snapshot of the ministry deacons performed in the early church. As the word deacon implies, they are servants of the church, particularly for physical needs.

Why would Paul mention the "overseers and deacons" in this letter? Why in a letter to the Philippian church? Hellerman surveys several plausible reasons for Paul to specifically address the leaders at Philippi.[12]

- Fortify the rightful leader's authority in the midst of opposition, e.g., 2:14-15.
- Demonstrate his high regard for them while challenging them to grow in their faith and leadership.
- These are the overseers who sent Epaphroditus to minister to Paul.

None of these reasons are mutually exclusive. Paul could have mentioned the "overseers and deacons" for all three reasons.

Note that the letter uses the phrase "with the overseers and deacons." Some assert a possible alternative translation of the text, "*fellow*-overseers and deacons," but this is generally regarded as because the address is primarily to the entire congregation, not just the congregation's leaders.

"Grace and Peace" (1:2)

Grace and peace may seem generic, but they are important. Grace (*charis*) was the typical greeting given in a Greco-Roman letter, whereas peace (*eirēnē*) was customary in Jewish greetings. However, Paul changes the typical Greek term for grace (*charin*) to a different term (*charis*) which makes this into a distinctively Christian greeting. He uses this greeting in six other letters (Romans, 1-2 Corinthians, Galatians, Ephesians, and Philemon).

INSIGHTS FROM THE TEXT

Leaders are Believers! The letter is addressed primarily to the saints, not to the leaders, overseers and deacons. That is our first designation as a leader in the church, a holy one. However, this does not mean that leaders are to be "holier than thou" in their relationship to the congregation. Rather, it reminds us that first and foremost, leaders, whether overseers or deacons, are to exhibit a spiritual maturity and have a growing relationship with Jesus Christ. In the church, not all believers are leaders, but all leaders must be believers!

Leaders Come From Within the Church! "The community as a whole is addressed, and in most cases therefore the 'overseers and deacons' are simply reckoned *as being within the community*. When they are singled out, as here, the leaders are not 'over' the church, but are addressed 'alongside of' the church, as a distinguishable part of the whole, *but as part of the whole, not above or outside it*."[13] One may have positional authority as a leader, with a title; but it takes time to become a leader within the church. Overseers and deacons are not outside appointees from some distant hierarchical or ecclesiastical authority, but are those who have matured and been recognized as leaders before assuming their function and role.

"Leaders" is Plural! Without overemphasizing the point, Paul does not write to the overseer and the deacon, but to overseers and deacons, plural. The church does not have a singular head or solo-leader in the New Testament, except Jesus Christ (Eph. 1:10, 22; 4:15; Col. 1:18). About 50 years after Paul wrote to the Philippians, an early church authority, Polycarp, wrote to the Philippian church and mentions they had a plurality of elders, *presbuteroi*.[14]

Overseers and Deacons are Leaders. In the New Testament, three terms are synonymous for the same function or role.

- *Episkopos* – overseer: noting the administrative, leader/manager function of church leaders

- *Presbuteros* – elder: highlighting the spiritual maturity of the leader, one who possesses Godly wisdom

- *Poimenos* – shepherd or pastor: emphasizing the one who cares for the flock of God, the function of nurturing, feeding, caring for, and protecting the flock (Acts 20:17-32). Note that the contemporary translation and title of "pastor" (Eph. 4:11) is in fact a transliteration of the Latin *pastores*, simply meaning *shepherd*.

This makes us ask, why does Paul choose *episkopos*? Some have suggested that the term would be familiar to any citizen of Philippi since it was used commonly to describe both civic and religious officials in Greek cities near Philippi.[15] However, it could be to emphasize and remind these leaders of their role as administrators, as overseers of the church.

If both overseers and deacons are church leaders, what is the difference? As one reads 1 Timothy 3, where the qualifications for both roles are provided, they are remarkably similar, almost identical. What is the difference between the leadership of overseers/elders and deacons? It is a difference of scope. Figure 1.4 illustrates the scope of leadership of the overseers and of the deacons.

Both overseers and deacons are leaders, and both should assume a posture of servant (as we will discuss in Chapter 4), but the distinction is the scope of their leadership. Overseers-elders-shepherds lead the whole flock, the entire church; whereas deacons serve the church through specific ministries within the church and community.

Figure 1.4

Paul knew the Philippians and Their Leaders. We do lead through relationships. It is difficult to lead, serve, shepherd, teach, or do ministry of any kind if we do not know those to whom we are ministering. The entire tone of Paul's introduction, as well as the remainder of his letter to the Philippian believers, is one of friendship. He knows with whom he is working and to whom he is ministering. He is familiar with the congregation, and they likewise know him, even his personal health and life challenges. Leaders can be transparent with congregations, to an extent, and this enables congregations to be transparent with their leaders.

PERSONAL & TEAM REFLECTION

1. How would you describe your personal relationship with Jesus Christ? What are some ways you could cultivate your relationship further as a believer and a leader-team?

2. How well do the elder team members relate to one another? What are some ways they could improve? What could you, individually or as a team, do to build a more resilient relationship?

3. How does your congregation define the relationship between overseers and deacons? How are their ministries different from one another in your congregation? What could be done to both strengthen the distinction and the collaboration between the overseers and deacons?

4. What are some ways you as a leader and as a group of the leaders, whether overseers or deacons, strengthen your relationship with the congregation? What might be some ways to be more "present" in the congregation?

Chapter 2

Partners vs. Opponents (1:3-18)

Yes, I am a UK fan! No, not the United Kingdom, the University of Kentucky Wildcats. Like most others from Kentucky, and especially from my hometown of Lexington, we all bleed blue. Nothing demonstrates this more than Big Blue Madness and the "Blue-White Scrimmage." The first public practice of the Wildcats is the Big Blue Madness, *at 12:01am*. Since 1982, UK has invited fans to Rupp Arena to celebrate the start of a new basketball season some fans camp out for days in hopes of getting *free tickets* for a first look at the Cats. In 2013, 755 tents were set up outside Rupp Arena in anticipation of the free ticket release. All 23,500 seats were taken within a matter of hours. The centerpiece of the Madness is the "Blue-White Scrimmage," when the Wildcats *play against themselves* in a scrimmage match. However, when it's time to play the real game, they have to cease scrimmaging and play as a team.

Objectively, UK's basketball team has one of the best records in history, especially among the SEC not just because of talented players, but because they are a *team*. Everyone knows that teams accomplish more than the sum of their collected parts; that's called synergy. Teams maximize one another's individual contributions to achieve more than thought possible. But what if some players still want to scrimmage? When do members of the team not behave like a team? They may be playing in the game, but they're not contributing to the team!

The apostle Paul had a team. He described the Philippians as his partners in the gospel and co-laborers in his ministry. They were his team. *However*, not everyone was a partner, not everybody was on his team. Paul did have his opponents in Philippi, both inside the church and in the community, who challenged his ministry, opportunists who saw an advantageous occasion with his incarceration. The questions for his leaders then, and for church leaders today, are simple: *Which team do you play on? Why are you playing the game?*

THE TEXT

Philippians 1:3-18 3 I thank my God in all my remembrance of you, 4 always in every prayer of mine for you all making my prayer with joy, 5 because of your partnership [*koinonia*] in the gospel from the first day until now. 6 And I am sure of this, that he who began a good work in you will bring it to completion at the day of Jesus Christ. 7 It is right for me to feel this way about you all, because I hold you in my heart, for you are all partakers with me of grace, both in my imprisonment and in the defense [*apologia*] and confirmation [*bebaiōsis*] of the gospel. 8 For God is my witness, how I yearn for you all with the affection [*splagchnon*] of Christ Jesus. 9 And it is my prayer that your love may abound more and more [*mǎllon kai mǎllon*], with knowledge and all discernment, 10 so that you may approve what is excellent, and so be pure and blameless for the day of Christ, 11 filled with the fruit of righteousness that comes through Jesus Christ, to the glory and praise of God.

12 I want you to know, brothers [*adelphoi*], that what has happened to me has really [*mǎllon*] served to advance [*prokopān*] the gospel, 13 so that it has become known throughout the whole imperial guard [*praitōriō*] and to all the rest that my imprisonment is for Christ. 14 And most of the brothers, having become confident in the Lord by my imprisonment, are much more bold to speak the word without fear.

15 Some indeed preach Christ from envy and rivalry, but others from good will. 16 The latter do it out of love, knowing that I am put here for the defense of the gospel. 17 The former proclaim Christ out of rivalry, not sincerely but thinking to afflict me in my imprisonment. 18 What then? Only that in every way, whether in pretense or in truth, Christ is proclaimed, and in that I rejoice.

TEXT QUESTIONS

- In Philippians 1:3, what does Paul say he does every time he remembers the Philippians?
- What do you think Paul means when he expresses his gratitude for the Philippians in v. 3, and how can we cultivate a similar attitude of thankfulness in our own lives?
- What specific reason does Paul give in Philippians 1:5 for his gratitude towards the Philippians?
- In Philippians 1:6, what confidence does Paul express regarding the Philippians' spiritual journey?
- How does Paul's confidence in God's work among the Philippians (v. 6) encourage you in your personal faith journey, especially during challenging times?
- How does Paul's prayer for the Philippians to grow in love and discernment (vv. 9-10) challenge us to consider what it means to truly love others in our own lives?
- What does Paul say in Philippians 1:12-13 about his imprisonment, and how has it affected the spread of the gospel?

INTO THE TEXT

Who were Paul's partners? Who were his opponents? As we move out of the salutation, we read a statement of affirmation, one of thankfulness and gratitude. Let's look at Paul's team!

Gratitude for Their Partnership (1:3-6)

Paul's remembrance of them for their consistent "partnership in the gospel" (v. 3) affirms them. This would not only speak of the congregation's general engagement, but the participation of the overseers and deacons, too. In regard to Philippians 1:3, Theodoret's (A.D. 392-428) commentary observed, "Paul praises God every time he remembers the clergy [overseers and deacons] of Philippi, who received the proclamation of the gospel cordially and have remained uncorrupted up to the present."[16] Paul also expresses his gratitude for their growth in the faith. A maturing faith is indeed an expectation for church leaders, whether overseers or deacons, and he has gratitude that they continue to progress in their relationship with Jesus Christ.

This passage introduces one of Philippians' major themes, containing the first reference to *joy* or *rejoice* (v. 4). In the immediate context, Paul emphasizes joy even in the presence of conflict, hardships, and his own imprisonment. William Barclay identifies ten reasons for "joy" found in Paul's letter to the Philippians![17] It is because of God's grace and peace that the Philippians experience their gratitude and joy. Paul rejoices in their partnership, advancing the gospel *together*.

Partnership in the Gospel vs. Personal Gain (1:5-6)

Paul reminds the Philippian leaders that their partnership in the gospel is a permanent priority (1:5), one that has been present in the congregation since its inception. This priority is not circumstantial (1:12). His imprisonment, or other hardships that they may encounter, do not deter it. For Paul, the gospel sees opportunities, not obstacles (1:13). Regardless of the circumstances, every situation was an opening to advance the gospel, emphasizing that their partnership in the gospel was of more significance than personal concerns, saying, "What then? Only that in every way, whether in pretense or in truth, Christ is proclaimed, and in that I rejoice" (Phil. 1:18).

Paul uses the word *koinonia* (1:5, 7; 2:1; 3:10; 4:14, 15), here translated *partnership*, to describe his relationship to the Philippian leaders. It was a word that described all kinds of relationships, both formal (such as marriage or business) or informal (friends), but always a quality of joint purpose and unified identity with one another. So, when Paul uses the word in his letter it requires definition, in this case, a *gospel partnership*![18] *Koinonia* is most frequently translated *fellowship*, and hence Paul speaks of a fellowship with the gospel. This is not just fellowship the way we think of it, like an after-church potluck dinner. It is more like the word fellowship used in *Lord of the Rings*, the *Fellowship of the Rings*. Fellowship here assumes a much deeper sense, reminding us that we are on a mission, we have a task to achieve; one that requires our whole engagement; not just financial support, but support in every possible way.

When Paul commends them for the "good work" in them (v. 6) it is crucial to note that it is not *their* good works, but the good work *only* God can do within them. It is what God started, probably their salvation, that they now share with others through evangelism, which is their participation in the gospel ministry. Paul recognizes the Philippians' achievements, but now reminds and emphasizes Christ's role in it. Augustine (A.D. 354-430), *On Grace and Free Will*, "God can work in our acts without our help. But when we will the deed, he cooperates with us."[19] The work of God in the life of the Philippian believers is comprehensive, spanning from the . . .

- Past ("began a good work in you")
- Present ("I am sure of this")
- Future ("will bring it to completion")

Barclay suggests that the Greek terms refer to the beginning and completion of a sacrifice, implying that the Christian life is one of perpetual sacrifice to Jesus Christ.[20] Indeed this is the sentiment of Paul when he wrote:

> I appeal to you therefore, brothers, by the mercies of God, to present your bodies as a living sacrifice, holy and acceptable to God, which is your spiritual worship. Do not be conformed to this world, but be transformed by the renewal of your mind, that by testing you may discern what is the will of God, what is good and acceptable and perfect (Rom. 12:1-2).

Completion means it has achieved its intended goal, once again, the advance of the gospel to others. When will this be completed? Ultimately, on the "day of Jesus Christ," most probably the second coming (Phil. 2:16; 1 Thes. 5:2-11; 2 Pet. 3:10-13; Rev. 20:11-21:8).

Affection (1:7-8)

Paul offers the Philippian believers no faint praise, but one that is sincere and rooted in his experience with them. Building on his previous statements, he now describes them as not only partners, but also "partakers with me of grace" (v. 7). He further delineates that they are partakers with him in his current imprisonment, and, once again, in the gospel; affirming the unity and relationship that existed between him and the congregation. Imprisonment in the ancient world placed inmates under perilous conditions, where often friends and family provided the daily necessities. Even if the imprisonment spoken of here is Paul's two-year "house arrest" in Rome (Acts 28:30-31), note that Paul had to provide it, and while others could visit, he could not leave.

Paul speaks in verse 7 of their "defense" [*apologia*] and "confirmation" [*bebaiōsis*] of the gospel. Both terms have a legal sense of an argument for innocence in the court that is founded on a solid legal precedent, reassuring his readers. It could also be taken more generally that Paul has always defended the gospel in every context due to his confidence in the gospel. Some have also noted that the use of *apologia* could indicate a Roman tribunal, like Paul was awaiting in Rome, his legal defense, but here it is certainly a defense of the gospel.

Continuing with his sincere praise of the Philippians, he expresses his affection and affirmation of their ministry. Verse 8 says, "how I *yearn* for you all . . . ", using a word that means straining after an object, or eagerness. Paul wants to see the Philippians again. In fact, *affection* is an understatement. Paul uses perhaps the strongest Greek term to convey his feelings toward the Philippians, *splagchnon* (v. 8). It literally means one's innermost parts, or specifically the bowels. Paul also uses it to describe his appreciation for Philemon (Phm. 7).

Prayer for the Philippians (1:9-11)

While prayer is a general practice, and often appears to be of general content; Paul always addressed the prayers in his epistles to the specific circumstance or individuals to whom it was written, even to the leaders here. Prayer for "caregivers" those who minster within the church, especially the leaders.

Paul, having provided the reason for his prayer (vv. 3-6) and expressed his affection for the Philippians, now expresses the content of his prayer in vv. 9-11. His prayer for the Philippians and their leaders has five items: (1) love abounding, (2) knowledge and discernment, (3) which results in a recognition of excellence, (4) their character ("pure and blameless"), and finally, (5) filled with Christ's righteousness. Certainly, this reflects not only his affection for the Philippians, but his desire for their continued formation as a congregation.

While it is not as evident in English, in verse 9 Paul prays that their love abounds, adding the phrase "more and more" which in Greek is "*mắllon kai mắllon*," emphasizing something going beyond the norm. He will use *mắllon* later in v. 12 in reference to the advancement of the gospel.

Speaking about their discernment, Paul uses a term that denotes an inner compass that can lead one to make moral decisions in spite of the fluid circumstances or the array of options presented. It is an inner perception, spiritual or moral, that has practical application.

Paul's desire for their character to be both "pure and blameless" as well as "righteous" takes on two dimensions. The first is in reference to how others perceive them, while the latter is in regard to their relationship with Jesus Christ. Paul's final two prayer items emphasize the believer's inner life as it relates to others (horizontal) and to Christ (vertical). "Pure" carries the meaning of being without mixture or having a singular composition, whereas "blameless" conveys the notion of one who spiritually walks without stumbling or causing others to do so.

When one hears the word "blameless," the core quality of an elder's and deacon's inner life, what perhaps comes to mind is "character." In Philippians, the quality of "blamelessness" is mentioned several times (1:10, 2:5, 3:6). Though written at least seven years prior to Paul's letters to Timothy, and perhaps shortly before the one to Titus, it underscores the necessity of an honorable character among church leaders – blameless, above reproach, an example – even though the same term is not used in Philippians as in 1 Timothy or Titus. Motyer describes the overseers' and deacons' relationship to one another and with the congregation itself as "leaders alongside" as a matter of character, writing, "That the leaders and those who are being led share an acknowledged commonality of being sinners saved by the same sacrifice of Christ, they were first church members of the same body, and that they share the same Christian experience; all of which would require them to "act with transparent integrity."[21]

Evangelism (1:12-14)

Twice in this passage, he addresses the *adelphoi*, translated brothers (vv. 12, 14). While the literal and basic meaning of the term is brothers, note that it can be used more figuratively as sisters, siblings; also, in context, it can mean "fellow Christians."[22] Paul reminds these co-workers that his current circumstances have already produced results for advancing the gospel. Like Joseph in Egypt (Gen. 39-40), God is at work in Paul's life and ministry even while he is imprisoned in Rome. Paul explains that the gospel has advanced (*prokopēn*), made forward progress, even while he was personally *restricted*. Paul reminds the Philippian leaders that evangelism, and the gospel ministry in general, occurs both inside prison and outside of prison; circumstances or context do not bind it.

It is easy to miss the parallel use of *mǎllon* here and later in Philippians 2:12, 23, and 3:4. But in the immediate context, it emphasizes how, in spite of our circumstances or events of our life, even those whom society deems unfitting, such as those in prison, we can "be confident that Christ will continue to use events in your life to bring about the knowledge of him in others, more and more."[23]

In the verses that follow (vv. 13-14), he presents a simple but profound principle: People are hearing the gospel (v. 13) because people are presenting the gospel (v. 14). Explaining what he has shared in the previous verses, Paul says that because of his imprisonment, some of the "imperial guard" have come to faith in Jesus Christ. He uses the formal term *praitōrion*, the Praetorian Guard, the Emperor's own personal guard, those who were often attached to the households of Roman officials. The term is rarely used outside of Rome and Italy, suggesting that Paul was probably in Rome. However, the gospel was not only appealing to the praetorians, but "to all the rest . . ." (v. 13). This could refer to the members of a typical Roman household (Eph. 5:21-6:10).

Here, Paul stresses the *results* of the imprisonment (1:13b-14). Unbelievers become believers (conversion) and believers become encouraged to be even more bold in sharing their faith (evangelism). However, his wording hints at the presence of opposition, opponents to his ministry. "*Most* of the brothers . . .," not all. Some were not encouraged by Paul's imprisonment. Not everyone in the Philippian congregation, *possibly* not all the leaders, were necessarily his partners.

Opposition from the Imprisonment

Luke describes Paul's imprisonment in Acts 28:20 as being bound in chains, and Paul says in Ephesians 6:20, that he associates his imprisonment with his service as an "ambassador in chains." How could his incarceration stir confidence in the believers, especially the church leaders? It didn't. Paul writes that his example encouraged "most" to become bolder in sharing their faith. Verse 14 attributes the Philippians' increased zeal to Paul's faithful endurance while undergoing imprisonment. While leaders were probably at first anxious for Paul and his circumstances, now they are encouraged to be bold, to take courage in their ministry. Some manuscripts specify that they are speaking God's Word, not just their own.[24] What is hinted at in verse 14 is fully expressed in the verses that follow.

Motives for Ministry (1:15-18)

Remember, for Paul, the advancement of the gospel was paramount, and the Philippians' participation in ministry was precious to him. This is underscored in vv. 15-17 where the gospel's advancement is a priority even over opposition, ill-will, and poor motivation for their ministry. "God is making good use of their bad intentions" (v. 16).[25] While both partners and opponents "preach Christ" (v. 15), their preaching is rooted in two radically opposite motives. Table 2.1 parallels the motives of Paul's opponents vs. his partners.

Opponents of Paul	Partners with Paul
"envy and rivalry" (v. 15a)	"good will" (v. 15b)
"not sincerely" (v. 17a)	"do it out of love" (v. 16a)
"to afflict me" (v. 17b)	"I am put here . . ." (v. 16b)

Table 2.1

Paul honors their partnership, as opposed to those who used his incarceration and temporary absence as a means of gaining power and prestige for themselves. Paul does not make the opposition about himself; he does not pose his partners against those who oppose him. Rather, he elevates Christ above both. Verse 18 reminds all his readers that it is preaching Christ that is preeminent, not him or them, no us versus them, but Christ over all. In turn, this causes us to assess our motivation for ministry, and ultimately ask, "Whom do we serve?" The interests of Christ or our own? Remember, for example, preaching out of "good will" is not just about their motivation, but also the outcomes of preaching with proper motivation.

What Do We Know About These Opponents?

This is crucial. Paul's description of their opposition, as well as his response to it, indicates several characteristics about them. First, his opponents are *Christians*. In context, he describes them as "brothers," and he never addresses them as otherwise. The opposition to his ministry, and that of the Philippians, is not just from outside the church, but some from within the Philippian congregation. Second, these opponents are *opportunistic*. They seek to make the most of Paul's absence, and the reason for his absence, his incarceration, and use it for personal advancement or gain. Third, they were *antagonists*. These opponents seem to express personal antagonism towards Paul. Gordon Fee says that the tone of vv. 15-17 indicate that some of the Philippians must "have personal animosity toward the apostle," not his message or teachings, but him.[26] This would be similar to what Paul experienced in Corinth, as Paul wrote in 1 Corinthians 1-2, and his engagement with the "super-apostles" in 2 Corinthians 11:5, but the Corinthian opposition was far more severe and not just personal. Finally, it's important to recognize that they are *not heretics*. They are never accused of preaching another, alternative gospel, such as in Galatians 1, and he does not condemn them as false teachers, as in the Corinthian correspondence, and even affirms the value of their work. Paul's principal concern was that we be on Christ's team, not his or his opponents' team. However, he makes it clear that, as a partner in the gospel, the church is united and Christ is proclaimed more effectively, to the benefit of all, rather than through a divisive or self-seeking messenger of the gospel. It is more advantageous for the church if you are partners with Paul in proclaiming the gospel from selfless motives. Paul elevates Christ above the conflict. No longer is the opposition a matter of horizontal connection, us versus them, but now has a vertical dimension, our relationship to Christ! "Only that in every way, whether in pretense or in truth, Christ is proclaimed, and in that I rejoice" (v. 18).

INSIGHTS FROM THE TEXT

As we reflect on the text, we see that Paul offers support of the believers and their leaders at Philippi, praise that is specific and well-deserved. He does not offer platitudes, but heartfelt acknowledgement of their partnership in the gospel ministry (1:3-11). Through his example, he then challenged them to make use of every occasion as an opportunity to share the gospel. What most would interpret as an impediment, his imprisonment, Paul used as a new opportunity to advance Christ's kingdom (1:12-18), and most of the Philippians partnered with him.

Leaders Prioritize Evangelism! Paul reminds us that evangelism is every believer's responsibility (v. 13). For Paul, "evangelism was his 'meat and potatoes'."[27] This is not only evident from his letter to the Philippian leaders, but his example when planting the church. Acts 16:12-40 contains the conversion accounts of Lydia and her household, a demon-possessed slave girl, as well as his jailer and his household, all within 28 verses! Consider the proclamation of the demonic slave girl, "These men are servants of the most high God, *who proclaim to you the way of salvation*" (Acts 16:17, emphasis added). Now Paul writes to the Philippians commending their partnership with him in the gospel (1:5), serving "side by side" (4:3), which was a feature unique to the congregation at Philippi (4:15). We are all called, especially the leaders of God's people, to defend and confirm the gospel (1:7, 15) and one way of accomplishing this is to advance it (1:12). *The power of the gospel is not merely in possessing it, but in professing it!*

Leaders' Reputations Matters. Yes, all believers should live lives that are qualitatively different from the culture and the community in which they live, and even more so for Christian leaders. Peter would remind us that, as Christians, we are to live "as sojourners and exiles to abstain from the passions of the flesh, which wage war against your soul. Keep your conduct among the Gentiles honorable, so that when they speak against you as evildoers, they may see your good deeds and glorify God on the day of visitation" (1 Pet. 2:11-12). Paul summarizes all this in one word: *blameless.*

But how do we describe this quality? In his letters to Timothy and Titus, Paul uses parallel terms and phrase "above reproach" (Titus 1:6), pointing to the matter of a leader's reputation in the church and the community, and Peter calls on leaders to be examples to the flock (1 Pet. 5:3), but what does it mean to be blameless? Figure 2.1 captures an approach to understanding an elder's or deacon's quality of blamelessness.[28]

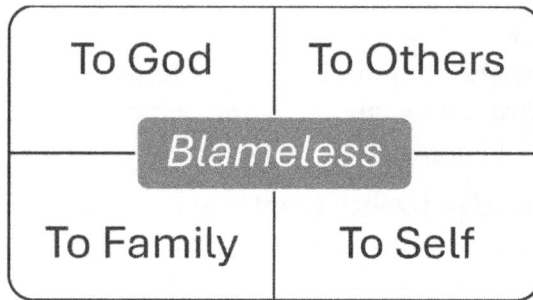

To God	To Others
Blameless	
To Family	To Self

Figure 2.1

Blameless toward whom? Leaders should be blameless before God (1 Pet. 5:2, 4; Titus 1:7-8; 1 Tim. 3:2, 9), such as having an orthodox faith. They should also be blameless before others (1 Tim. 3:2, 3, 7-8, 11, 13; Titus 1:7-8; 1 Pet. 5:2-3), which speaks to a leader's reputation. Likewise, leaders should be blameless before their family, especially in regard to their spouse and children (1 Tim. 3:2, 4, 12; Titus 1:6), and how the family functions together (1 Tim. 3:4-5; Titus 1:6). Finally, a leader must be blameless before themselves, having a clear conscience (1 Tim. 3:2-3, 9; Titus 1:7). All of this assumes that a leader in the church has been vetted (1 Pet. 5:2, 1 Tim. 3:1), or as Paul writes about leaders, "Let them also be tested first; then let them serve as deacons if they prove themselves blameless" (1 Tim. 3:10).

Even Good Leaders Face Opposition. Philippians is often regarded as a model church, one that, unlike Corinth, gave Paul great joy. Paul even visited it a second time (Acts 20), not due to corrective action, such as his ill-fated visits to Corinth, but because of pastoral necessity. He knew the believers in Philippi would be there for him in his time of need. However, his letter to the Philippians reminds church leaders that even in the best of congregations and circumstances, opposition and division is always present. It is not a matter of whether opposition is present or absent, but simply to what degree is it present and prevalent. Philippians teaches us that leaders will always be on the forefront of addressing conflict and opposition, even in the most favorable circumstances and in mature congregations. Even while the vast majority may be cheering, remember there will always be a group even in the church that is gloomy and loathsome.

Prayer is Essential for Leaders. Paul starts this passage with his prayer for the Philippians and their leaders. He stands as an example and reminder that leaders pray for *everything* and *everyone*. Paul's prayers were specific and tailored to the individual, group, or circumstance in which he ministered. In this way, voicing a prayer was indeed an encouragement to those hearing it, or reading it in his letter. In this paragraph, the totality of prayer cannot possibly be addressed. But, one matter should be identified that is all too common for leadership teams in the church. Prayer is seen as perfunctory, ritual, something to do to start a meeting. "Well, let's pray and then get down to the agenda . . . ." Prayer IS part of the agenda. Prayer IS part of a church leader's ministry. Prayer IS a preliminary before anything else can be done. It needs to become more than the routine used to open the meeting.

Leaders Encourage Others. Remember the opening of the epistle? To whom it was addressed? It was to the entire congregation *"with* overseers and deacons" (1:1). They are partners, leading from alongside, not over. Paul empowers the leaders of the Philippian congregation so that they too may encourage and empower others to partner alongside them in the gospel ministry (1:3-11). In short, to serve as a *team*! Leaders are not required to do everything, and in fact cannot do everything, but they encourage and empower others in the congregation to use their gifts, talents, abilities, and resources to advance the gospel as partners in ministry.

PERSONAL & TEAM REFLECTION

1. Joy/Rejoice. Divide into two teams. Team 1 reads the passages in the left column and Team 2 reads the passages in the right column. Simply identify what brings Paul joy and/or for what he is rejoicing in each passage.

Team 1	Team 2
1:4	2:28
1:18	2:29
1:25	3:1
2:2	4:1
2:17-18	4:4
	4:10

   Based on the above exercise, how well would your congregation bring Paul joy or rejoicing? Explain your response.

2. What kind of opposition has your leadership team experienced? What was the source of the opposition? How well did your leadership team address it? In what way was Christ elevated above the conflict, as Paul did in 1:18?

3. Can you identify 3 ways you could partner better together as leaders for the advance of the gospel, that is, evangelism and outreach?

4. In regard to blamelessness, how does your leadership team "vet" or "onboard" new leaders? How is a potential leader's character assessed?

5. How could your leadership team engage in prayer more effectively? Consider 3 ways you could improve your leadership team's prayer life.

Chapter 3

Worthily vs. Worldly (1:19-30)

In 1980, spokesperson Ricardo Montalbán introduced the world to the new Chrysler luxury line, featuring the Cordoba. The Chrysler Cordoba was technologically more advanced than its competitors and featured unparalleled amenities. While filming the now-iconic commercial, he was supposed to describe the car as having "seats made of high-grade vinyl" but Montalbán asked for a retake. He then introduced the Cordoba as having luxurious seats made of "soft Corinthian leather." This catch phrase was then used to market Chrysler's luxury line throughout the 1980s. What is "soft Corinthian leather"? Nothing more than high grade vinyl. In fact, Ricardo Montalbán coined the phrase. It didn't exist when he said it, and technically it still doesn't exist. It's just vinyl! Regardless of what you called the material, it remained just fake leather, vinyl. Yet, the revised description helped sell hundreds of thousands of Cordobas. In fact, the existence of "Corinthian leather" was echoed on such shows as WKRP in the 1980s and Seinfeld in the 1990s. The label stuck!

This shows how the world places a premium on form over substance, appearances over reality. Remember the Billy Crystal skit on Saturday Night Live, impersonating Fernando Lamas? "It's now how you feel, it's how you look, and you look marvelous!" Even leaders are tempted to emphasize only the surface traits of a leader in the absence of any significant spiritual depth or actual abilities.

Does this work in the church? Christian leaders place a premium on their inner life, rather than the trappings of leadership. Paul urges the Philippians and their leaders to live lives worthily of the gospel, while their opponents are not. It is a matter of *substance*. What we are really "made of." Are you genuine? Or, as Paul would say, are you walking worthily or worldly?

THE TEXT

Philippians 1:18-30 18 Yes, and I will rejoice, 19 for I know that through your prayers and the help of the Spirit of Jesus Christ this will turn out for my deliverance, 20 as it is my eager expectation [*apokaradokia*] and hope that I will not be at all ashamed, but that with full courage now as always Christ will be honored in my body, whether by life or by death. 21 For to me to live is Christ, and to die is gain. 22 If I am to live in the flesh, that means fruitful labor for me. Yet which I shall choose I cannot tell. 23 I am hard pressed between the two. My desire is to depart [*analusai*] and be with Christ, for that is far better. 24 But to remain in the flesh is more necessary on your account. 25 Convinced of this, I know that I will remain and continue with you all, for your progress and joy in the faith, 26 so that in me you may have ample cause to glory in Christ Jesus, because of my coming to you again.

27 Only let your manner of life [*politeuesthai*, literally "citizen"] be worthy of the gospel of Christ, so that whether I come and see you or am absent, I may hear of you that you are standing firm in one spirit, with one mind striving side by side for the faith of the gospel, 28 and not frightened in anything by your opponents. This is a clear sign to them of their destruction [*apōleia*], but of your salvation, and that from God. 29 For it has been granted to you that for the sake of Christ you should not only believe in him but also suffer for his sake, 30 engaged in the same conflict that you saw I had and now hear that I still have.

TEXT QUESTIONS

- In Philippians 1:19, what does Paul say will lead to his deliverance?
- What do you think Paul means when he says, "to live is Christ and to die is gain" (1:21), and how can this perspective influence our priorities and choices in life and as a leader?

- What dilemma does Paul express in Philippians 1:22-23 regarding whether he desires to live or die?
- According to Philippians 1:27, how does Paul urge the Philippians to conduct themselves?
- How can we apply Paul's encouragement to stand firm in one spirit and strive together for the faith of the gospel (1:27) in our own congregation and communities?

INTO THE TEXT

Paul once again returns to the theme of joy/rejoice in his regard for the Philippian believers. His rejoicing is based on their partnership in the gospel and the proclamation of the Good News, which closed our previous section (v. 18). Paul now turns his attention to the character of a ministry partner, the inner life of the leader.

Prayer for Deliverance (1:19-21)

William Barclay reminds us that, "Paul was never too big a man to remember that he needed the prayers of his friends. . . . We cannot call a man our friend unless we pray for him."[29] Paul's mind is focused on his current situation, the circumstances of his imprisonment, awaiting his deliverance and possible reunion with the Philippians. He writes to them of his impending deliverance (v. 19), which is to be achieved through the Philippians' prayers on his behalf for the help of "the Spirit of Jesus Christ."

Paul is hopeful for deliverance (v. 20) from his circumstances based on the Philippians' prayers. In fact, he may have actually coined the term translated "eager expectation," Greek *apokaradokia*, to emphasize the situation.[30] Regardless, Paul affirms that he is "not at all ashamed" and lives "with full courage *as always.*" Consider this, if you learned that a friend or colleague, someone you knew closely, was now incarcerated, how would you respond? Would you treat them differently? Here Paul lets his supporters among the Philippian Christians know that he is the same Paul he has always been and there is no reason to shun him or regard him with disdain. He asserts that "Christ will be honored *in my body,*" adding that this is true whether he lives or dies, as long as it is for Christ. His witness is consistent whether it is "by life or by death." The section concludes with a familiar refrain, "For to me to live is Christ and to die is gain" (v. 21). Leaders, like Paul, live consistent lives, regardless of the situation; even in matters of life or death, Christ is at the center.

Two Desires (1:22-26)

Building off his previous affirmation of faithfulness in the face of life or death, Paul shares an internal struggle with the Philippians, one that he has certainly faced numerous times in his ministry and missionary journeys. For Paul, being with Jesus is the ultimate objective of the Christian life. So, should he desire to die to be with Christ in eternity now, or continue to live here and now for Christ? One benefits him, the other benefits the Philippians. Which should be his preferred future? Death or life?

Paul lets the Philippians into his inner world, the decision that weighs upon him. On the one hand, is it better to die and depart this world, which would let him be with Christ, which would indeed be better for Paul himself (v. 23)? Paul's choice of the word translated *depart* [*analusai*] demonstrates the seriousness of this matter. It is a vivid term signifying moving an encampment, leaving a harbor, or solving a riddle. In short, Paul is asking "Is it time for me to move on from this life to the next?" On the other hand, should he remain in this life, live in the flesh, which is better for the Philippians (v. 24)? From a leadership perspective, as a leader, do I do what is in my personal best interest, in this case depart this life to be with Christ in eternity, or do I place the benefits of others above or before my self-interests, continue in this life to serve the church? Remember, Paul is in prison with no sure outcome to his future. Should he be praying for a faithful death or a faithful life, for judgment or for release from his imprisonment? Merida and Chan describe this section as a "life worth living and a death worth dying."[31]

Paul answers the question for us, saying "Convinced of this . . ." (v. 25-26), it is more advantageous for the church that he stays and continue to serve. He explains that the preferred path forward is to remain with them, to continue to serve. Why? Paul recognizes their continued faith formation, the "progress and joy in the faith" (v. 25) he has witnessed among the Philippians. He reminds them that his release and continued ministry with them would give "cause to glory in Christ Jesus" (v. 26), not to mention that upon his release he intended to return to Philippi for a season of ministry.

Genuine Discipleship (1:27-30)

Dietrich Bonhoeffer, the German theologian and pastor who openly opposed Adolph Hitler to the point of his imprisonment and eventual death in a Nazi concentration camp, wrote a book that is as relevant today as it was in 1937. The book is, *The Cost of Discipleship*, based principally on Christ's Sermon on the Mount. In the opening section, Bonhoeffer juxtaposes cheap grace and costly grace, each with its distinct degree of discipleship, to what extent and the level of expectations regarding how one actually follows Jesus in our lives. Cheap grace is salvation without any expectation of discipleship; justification without sanctification. Costly grace recognizes Jesus alone saves us, but that salvation calls us to make a significant commitment to a new life; it will cost us our lives to live for Jesus. These words and the distinction they represent are not mere platitudes or sermonizing for Bonhoeffer. Remember that his own discipleship, following Christ, cost him his life.

Paul now issues a call to the Philippians for genuine discipleship, based on what Bonhoeffer would describe as costly grace. Paul urges the Philippians, and their leaders, to "behave as citizens worthy" (1:27a). The ESV translates this as "walk of life," but the term *politeuesthai* clearly implies citizenship, as in Philippians 3:20.

As a Roman, Paul was well aware of the value of citizenship, having appealed to it on numerous occasions to escape peril (Acts 16:37-38, 22:25-29, 23:27), and even employing it figuratively in a spiritual sense (Eph. 2:12, 19). Acts 16:11-40 details Paul's engagement with the Roman legal establishment in Philippi, and his incarceration in a Roman jail in Philippi.

Paul reminds the Philippians, and us, that the Christian faith is *more* than salvation! As my home preacher, Wally Rendel, once said, "Being a Christian is *more* than eternal fire insurance." Paul encourages them to live a life that is distinctively Christian, recognizable to all those who see it. That is why Philippians 1:27 and 3:2 use the same word translated *citizenship*, meaning a distinctive way of life. Are you going to live life as a Roman or as a Christian? Even if you say, "Both!" which one takes priority? Which receives your first allegiance?

I have had the pleasure of teaching internationally. I've taught throughout China, Heiligenkreuz, Austria (near Vienna), and on Prince Edward Island in Canada. In every instance, it was fairly easy to spot that I was a foreigner. In China, in addition to the obvious physical differences, I didn't speak or read Chinese and couldn't use chopsticks, always requesting a fork. Ah, a Westerner! In Austria, my United States nationality was discovered at, of all places, McDonalds in the Vienna airport. I wanted a quarter pounder with cheese. I scanned the display menu, and while I'm not fluent in German, I saw nothing that looked like a quarter pounder. Eventually, an adolescent lady behind the McDonalds counter got my attention and asked, "Are you an American?" "Yes." "Are you looking for the Quarter Pounder?" "Yes! How did you know?" "It's the Burger Royale. We are on the metric system. We don't have pounds." What about Canada? While we are neighbors in North America, we are culturally distinct. Our pronunciation of simple words, cultural phrases, loonies ($1 coin) and toonies ($2 coins) not to mention Canadians' fondness for *poutine*, which is an amazing dish. Once again, my awkwardness in purchasing items with a foreign currency, ordering off a menu of *poutines*, and pronouncing "sorry" as "soh-ry" all indicated I was not from the island. Honestly, this happens in the United States! I moved from central Illinois to Georgia. When I ordered unsweetened iced tea at a restaurant, they knew I was not from around there. Paul is saying to us that our manner of living, as a believer, should stand out, be recognized, get the curious stare, be different from the world. This is why Peter calls us "sojourners and exiles" in this world (1 Pet. 2:11).

Our commitment to living a life worthy of Christ, distinct from the world, is unconditional compulsion (v. 27b), regardless of the circumstances or the presence or absence of a person, in this case, Paul. What is one indicator of that life? One benchmark of living as a kingdom citizen? Unity. Paul stresses that the Philippians are *one* in spirit and mind, for the gospel. The unity of believers, their single vision in life is indeed a threat to those who walk on a different path. He acknowledges the opposition they have encountered, the opponents that challenge them in Philippi and himself in Rome (v. 28a). However, the destruction his opponents desire for him and the church at Philippi will actually be visited upon them. Their opposition will lead to their own destruction (*apōleia*) (v. 28b), but to the church's salvation (v. 28c). What is Paul saying? Persecution is indeed inevitable, we cannot avoid or escape it; but God offers sustaining grace to the faithful, those who continue to walk worthily of Christ.

Believe and Suffer (1:29-30)

For many, this verse is counter intuitive, it makes no sense. If we believe, we are going to suffer? Shouldn't believers have some special provision and protection from God against suffering, especially from suffering for the faith? Paul would say the opposite. He uses the word *granted*, or *given*. We are granted to believe in Christ and we are granted to suffer for Christ. Literally translated, v. 29 reads, "Because to you it was given *on behalf* of Christ not only to believe in him but also *on behalf* of him to suffer . . ." We believe and suffer on behalf of Christ! God granting this to us makes it a gift and a privilege to do so (see Matthew 5:10-12; Acts 5:41). In regard to our salvation, John uses a similar image in John 1:12, "But to all who did receive him, who believed in his name, *he gave the right* to become children of God." Paul continues to remind the Philippians and us that salvation is not earned or negotiated, it is not given because of works or based on our satisfaction. Both our salvation and suffering are "for the sake of Christ."

What kind of suffering? Paul describes it as a conflict that he has *previously* encountered and the Philippians *now* face themselves. In v. 30, he uses the phrase the "conflict that you saw" (when Paul was in Philippi) and the conflict you "now hear" (when Paul was currently in Rome). Conflict for the Philippians was not a hypothetical or abstract circumstance, but a reality of which they were fully aware. Don't forget who is writing this letter! It's not just Paul, the Apostle. This is Paul, their friend, sharer of the gospel, founder of their congregation, co-laborer in Christ, spiritual leader and father, and one suffering under house confinement in Rome for the sake of Christ. When Paul unites belief and suffering, this is not abstract or theoretical, it's reality for him.

INSIGHTS FROM THE TEXT

As leaders, are our lives worthy of Christ, or still reflecting worldly values and postures toward leadership? How can we be sure to posture ourselves as Christian leaders and reflect the values Christ would have us display to the world and other believers? Paul is saying that the body of Christ does not need worldly leaders, infecting it with a virus, but leaders who walk worthily of the name Christian.

Leaders Live the Gospel. *Not* lifestyle evangelism, we cannot present the gospel with just our example and nonverbal witness. Evangelism requires a voice! *But* our voice must be matched with a consistent witness! We live the gospel we proclaim, in both word and deed. We see this trait throughout the Philippian church. Lydia, the first Christian convert in Philippi and all of Europe, was "faithful to the Lord" (Acts 16:15). The jailer "rejoiced" that his family "believed in God" (Acts 16:34). Paul's repeated visits to Philippi testify to their witness, along with what he writes in his letter (Acts 20:12). Not only his letter to the Philippians, but Paul is probably alluding to the Philippians in 2 Corinthians 8:1-2 where he says, "We want you to know, brothers, about the grace of God that has been given among the churches of Macedonia, for in a severe test of affliction, their abundance of joy and their extreme poverty have overflowed in a wealth of generosity on their part." The Philippian congregation seems to reflect this praise. What's the point? Words can only take us so far in evangelism. Our lifestyle, our example, reinforces our words. As leaders, our example is paramount in not only evangelism, but encouraging other believers to share their faith. Living the gospel is more than just an encouragement to have a growing relationship with Jesus; it's about letting that relationship stimulate others in the congregation and becoming a witness to those seeking Christ.

Leaders Live in Paradox. Part of living worthily and not worldly is to navigate between our lives as Kingdom citizens and our lives as earthly citizens. An unavoidable tension exists trying to live as a citizen of heaven while still alive in an earthly nation. Where should the focus in our lives be? Here/Now versus There/Future, Christ Kingdom or current country, or Both/And? *Paradox*! How does this apply to leaders in the church?

First, all believers face these choices every day. As leaders, we need to set the example of how to navigate between being a genuine believer in Christ and a citizen of the United States (or Canada, or Austria, or Mexico, etc.). Second, as leaders, it is easy to lean primarily or too heavily on modern business practices of leadership rather than the principles of Scripture. Don't misunderstand the point. We can learn from sound business practices, but when we prioritize them over Scripture, we turn the church into a business rather than an embassy of heaven on a mission. Once again, that's the paradox, building a ministry that is faithful to Scripture, but also relevant in the 21st century. We live in that paradox! We hear it in the prayer of Jesus in the Garden:

> I have given them your word, and the world has hated them because they are not of the world, just as I am not of the world. I do not ask that you take them out of the world, but that you keep them from the evil one. They are not of the world, just as I am not of the world. Sanctify them in the truth; your word is truth. As you sent me into the world, so I have sent them into the world. And for their sake I consecrate myself, that they also may be sanctified in truth (Jn 17:14–19).

Remember Paul's conflict about remaining in this world or entering eternity? As leaders, we navigate in the paradox between living in eternity while still on earth! How do we live distinctive lives, worthy of the gospel, while not living so distinctly that we distract or dissuade people from the gospel?

Leaders Live Consistent Lives. Perhaps the previous question is best answered with this observation. Leaders need to live lives of consistency, demonstrating a commitment to Christ regardless of their current circumstances. Lives that are exemplars of the gospel in everyday encounters. Consistency is the key to living in a life of paradox. What is the alternative? Vacillating between the two opposites of Scripture and culture, irrelevant to relevant, reverent to irreverent, inconsistent witness and unstable lives.

Leaders have to set the example to help believers and congregations live consistently. No one can do it perfectly, but they can articulate a consistent rationale for their actions, explaining a common thread of faithful reasoning for their decisions and actions.

Leaders Permeate Ministry with Prayer. Previous chapters have already identified this as a leadership trait, but its reoccurrence throughout Philippians underscores its importance. Also, perhaps many in church leadership underutilize prayer and are indifferent to it. "Let's start the meeting, oh, let's pray first so we can get down to business." "Well, it's time to close, perhaps we should end in prayer." Prayer needs to be more than an opening or closing item on a leadership agenda. Prayer needs to be the business of the meeting. Prayer needs to permeate every item on the agenda. Prayer needs to be part of the follow-up to the meeting. Just a reminder, worldly leaders *don't* pray. Are we leading worthily or worldly?

Leaders Encounter Opposition from Outside. Unfortunately, leaders are too familiar with conflict *in* the church. However, Paul's letter to the Philippians reminds us today that conflict can come from outside the church. The more counter-cultural the church becomes, the more distinct from its environment, the more "worthy" than "worldly," opposition to their very presence is inevitable. This kind of opposition is often subtle and may go unnoticed. The proud Roman heritage of the colony in Philippi, tied to the imperial cult itself, retired legionnaires, now our identity as citizens is challenged, changed; Christian first, then Roman. Putting it in our terms, we are first Christian, then, what identity do you hold sacred? Nationality? Veteran? Political affiliation? Academic title? Paul would warn us just as Jesus did, "If you were of the world, the world would love you as its own; but because you are not of the world, but I chose you out of the world, therefore the world hates you" (John 15:19).

PERSONAL & TEAM REFLECTION

1. What experiences have you had with "persecution" (regardless of how slight) about your faith?

2. How consistent is your witness? Are there circumstances where it wanes or waivers? If so, when and why?

3. What has been the "cost" of being a Jesus-follower have you experienced?

4. Identify 3 ways your leadership team could better "permeate" your meetings with prayer.

5. What is one improvement you could make to your own prayer life?

Chapter 4

Same Mind vs. Grumbling Opposition (2:1-18)

Theodore Roosevelt, 26th President of the United States, was asked to speak on citizenship in a republic while traveling abroad. On April 23, 1910 he delivered one of his most memorable speeches at the Sorbonne in Paris, France. For this speech he penned, "The Man in the Arena," which contains one of his most impactful comments:

> The poorest way to face life is to face it with a sneer. There are many men who feel a kind of twisted pride in cynicism; *there are many who confine themselves to criticism of the way others do what they themselves dare not even attempt.* There is no more unhealthy being, no man less worthy of respect, than he who either really holds, or feigns to hold, *an attitude of sneering disbelief toward all that is great and lofty*, whether in achievement or in that noble effort which, even if it fails, comes second to achievement. . . . *It is not the critic who counts; not the man who points out how the strong man stumbles, or where the doer of deeds could have done them better.* The credit belongs to the man who is actually in the arena, whose face is marred by dust and sweat and blood; who strives valiantly; who errs, who comes short again and again, because there is no effort without error and shortcoming; but who does actually strive to do the deeds; who knows the great enthusiasms, the great devotions; who spends himself in a worthy cause; who at the best knows in the end the triumph of high achievement, and who at the worst, if he fails, at least fails while daring greatly, *so that his place shall never be with those cold and timid souls who neither know victory nor defeat.*[32]

I have this quote on the wall of my home study. Leaders lead, but never without the distraction of critics, cynics, complainers, and grumblers. Throughout the Scriptures, every leader had their naysayers. "The whole congregation of the people of Israel grumbled against Moses and Aaron" (Ex. 16:2), The people grumbled against Samuel for not giving them a king (1 Sam. 8:7). Shimei openly mocked and cursed David (2 Sam. 16:5ff), Tobiah and Ammon, doing Sanballat's bidding, challenged Nehemiah (Neh. 4:1-3ff). Even his own disciples grumbled against Jesus (Jn. 6:59-67). Now, Paul identifies grumblers in Philippi.

Previously, Paul described the Philippians as partakers and partners in the gospel, committed to evangelism and ministry, essentially part of his team. Now, he urges them, especially their leaders, to not grow distracted, but be like-minded. But he acknowledges the presence of dissenters, those who are *not* like-minded, who grumble, distract, and draw attention away from the ministry to which his co-laborers have committed.

In every congregation there are those who promote unity within the church and those who promote dissension. Unity in Christ is not simply the absence of grumbling, but growth despite it. Likewise, unity not simply because of external opposition, like the old Arabic saying, "the enemy of my enemy is my friend," but a cohesive unity based on factors within the faith community. It is an attitude of being like-minded, having the mind-of-Christ posture toward leadership rather than a self-centered posture of dissension in the church. For us, what do we bring to the leadership table? One that promotes unity through elevating Christ and drawing all closer to Him, or one who embraces cynicism and self-promotion, forging division?

THE TEXT

Philippians 2:1-18 1 So if there is any encouragement in Christ, any comfort from love, any participation in the Spirit, any affection and sympathy, 2 complete my joy by being of the same mind [*phroneō*], having the same love, being in full accord [*sumpsuchoi*] and of one mind [*phroneō*]. 3 Do nothing from rivalry or conceit, but in humility count others more significant than yourselves. 4 Let each of you look not only to his own interests, but also to the interests of others. 5 Have this mind [*phroneō*] among yourselves, which is yours in Christ Jesus, 6 who, though he was in the form of God, did not count equality with God a thing to be grasped, 7 but made himself nothing [kenōsis], taking the form of a servant, being born in the likeness of men. 8 And being found in human form, he humbled himself by becoming obedient to the point of death, even death on a cross. 9 Therefore God has highly exalted him and bestowed on him the name that is above every name, 10 so that at the name of Jesus every knee should bow, in heaven and on earth and under the earth, 11 and every tongue confess that Jesus Christ is Lord [kyrios], to the glory of God the Father.

12 Therefore, my beloved, as you have always obeyed, so now, not only as in my presence but much more in my absence, work out [katergazesthai] your own salvation with fear and trembling, 13 for it is God who works in you, both to will and to work for his good pleasure.

14 Do all things without grumbling [gŏggusmos] or questioning [dialogismos], 15 that you may be blameless and innocent, children of God without blemish in the midst of a crooked and twisted generation, among whom you shine as lights in the world, 16 holding fast to the word of life, so that in the day of Christ I may be proud that I did not run in vain or labor in vain. 17 Even if I am to be poured out as a drink offering upon the sacrificial offering of your faith, I am glad and rejoice with you all. 18 Likewise you also should be glad and rejoice with me.

TEXT QUESTIONS

- What does Paul encourage the Philippians to have in 2:2 to make his joy complete?
- In what ways does Paul's exhortation to consider others more significant than ourselves (v. 3) challenge the societal norms and expectations of contemporary leadership?
- How can the example of Christ's humility and sacrificial love described in vv. 5-8 influence our attitude and action toward others whom we lead?

- What does Paul say God did for Jesus in Philippians 2:9-11 after His humble obedience?
- What does Paul mean by working out our salvation with fear and trembling (v. 12) and how can this understanding guide our spiritual growth as leaders?
- In Philippians 2:14-15, how does Paul instruct the Philippians to behave, and what result does he expect from their conduct?

INTO THE TEXT

Fee described Philippians 1:12-26 as a letter of friendship, but *now* he regards this section as a letter of exhortation, challenging the Philippians, making an appeal, for them to accomplish something new.[33] In context, Paul is voicing concern that disunity and conflict within the church will distract us from sharing the gospel and sullies the witness of the church. "The gospel is all about reconciliation, and unreconciled people do not advertise it well."[34]

In this portion of his letter, Paul urges the Philippian congregation to be of the same mind, but more so their leadership. If a congregation's leaders are not of the same mind, the congregation will, in all probability, not be either. Paul promotes unity versus dissention in the congregation and its leadership (2:9-18). How? He first openly appeals to them to have the "same mind . . . Love, being in full accord and of one mind" (2:1-2). To do this, he reminds them of their role as humble servants of all (2:3-4), based on reflecting the mind of Christ (2:5-11), and continued progress in living out their new life in Christ (2:12-18). Essentially, the more Christlike we become, the more unified we will be due to having a posture of servant-leadership.

Motive Matters (2:1-4)

Paul recognizes three causes threatening the Philippians' unity: personal drive, desire for personal celebrity, and most obviously, self-centeredness (2:3-4). However, these three causes are simply sprouts from a common root: the elevation of the *self* over everything else.

If leaders are to be unified, they have to overcome the corrosive tendency to self-centeredness rather than being mission-driven.

Paul makes a personal appeal to the Philippians to "complete my joy" (2:1-2a)? How? He explains, "by being of the *same* mind [*phroneō*], having the *same* love, being in *full* accord [*sumpsuchoi*] and of *one* mind [*phroneō*]" (2:2b). How does a plurality of overseers and deacons please Paul? When they lead, serve, and work as one. They may be plural in number, but are to be singular in mind.

Paul uses the word *think* twice in v. 2 and again once in v. 5, translated *mind*. Emphasizing that the mind Paul wants us to have is the same as what was in Christ's mind, think like him (2:5)! The word we translate *mind* is a verb in Greek, *phroneō*, not a noun. Paul is saying to think like Jesus, a continual process your thinking, being like he did; it's a process, not just a product. He is encouraging, even challenging, the Philippians and their leaders to approach life with humility, allow humility to define their thinking. He also calls them to be of "one accord" (*sumpsuchio*), meaning of the same spirit, joined in soul, which speaks to the substance of their *relationship* as believers and leaders in the mission of Christ's church.[35] The inscription on an ancient pagan tombstone stresses the relational element: "We spoke the same things, we thought the same things, and we go the inseparable way in Hades."[36] The sentiment says it all. They were of one accord!

But why? Why is it so crucial that leaders and God's people be of one mind, accord, and love? Because to advance the gospel, to carry out the mission of the church, to genuinely serve as Christian leaders, requires humble, serving relationships (2:3-4). Verses 3-4 underscores humanity's brokenness, that our default is to act out of "rivalry and conceit" and to put our own needs first, both of which are counter to humility and unity. Verse 3 highlights one's inability and insufficiency in light of God's presence and power, not our own. As we look forward to verse 2:14, we find that grumbling and questioning are rooted here! Paul is telling leaders to cut such dissention off at its source, at the root. We can only put the needs of others before our own needs when we posture ourselves as a servant, realizing that it's not about us. What example could Paul provide the Philippian leaders for this kind of servant leadership? Jesus Christ.

Christ Our Example (2:5-11)

What is the purpose of this passage? Far too often it has been the focus of theological debate regarding the nature of Jesus, his divinity and humanity. But, was this the reason Paul penned the passage, to serve as a Christological statement? Yes, the passage does reference Jesus' pre-existence, the incarnation, his death, resurrection, ascension, and glorification; and all of this is predicated on a Trinitarian context in the previous verses (2:1-4). Figure 4.1 is based on a figure in Merida and Chan's commentary, signifying what this passage actually states about Jesus Christ.[37]

But, was this Paul intended message? Without a doubt these elements are crucial to the meaning of the passage, but Paul is speaking to the Philippian leaders, calling them to humble selfless service, as he indicates in verse 4. Paul opens the passage writing, "have this mind among yourselves, which is yours in Christ Jesus" (v. 5). Possessing this attitude will enable one to serve the interests of others, just as Christ Jesus did. Leaders who are Christian serve like Jesus. Hargrove regards this as "the Christ hymn as a song for leaders."[38] A hymn? Yes, the early church had what we would call hymns! Is this passage really a hymn? Many think so! It has a poetic structure, theology is often the subject of hymns, and it offers a summation of the New Testament's teaching on Jesus as both divine and human.

Kenōsis? (2:6-7) However, Paul uses the person of Jesus as our model for selfless leadership, and his statements are theologically rich. One term that has been a sticking point for many theologians is what exactly does it mean that Jesus "emptied" himself? What did he lose, leave behind, let go of? The passage itself affirms his divinity (v. 6) and yet also his humanity (v. 7). But how is this possible? This is the crux of the theological controversy. Most modern liberal Protestants, beginning in 19th century Germany, understood it to signify the loss of divine attributes,[39] but Catholic, Orthodox, traditional Protestantism, and modern evangelicals have *historically* regarded the *emptying* as not a loss, but as taking on human nature; being no longer purely divine. The "emptying" is not regarded as a loss of any divine attributes, but rather becoming human so as to exemplify his love for us and making his sacrifice on the cross possible.[40]

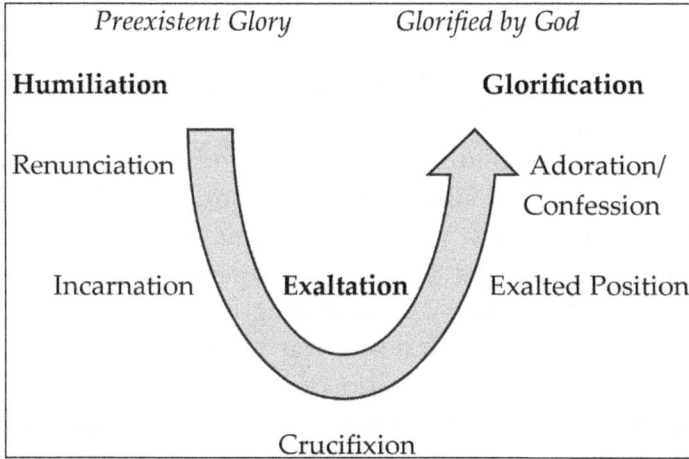

Figure 4.1

Paul's intention was to remind leaders that Christ was a servant, placing the needs of others before his own, just as Jesus did when he emptied himself by "taking the form of a servant" (2:7).

Why Did the Savior Have To Be Human (v. 8)? If Jesus had not been human, he could not have been an example of humble service toward others (v. 8a), nor could he have accomplished his work on the cross, his crucifixion and death (v. 8b). It should be noted that while verse 8 highlights Jesus' humanity, 2:11 has a cloaked reference to his divinity, one that contemporary readers often miss, but not its first century readers. Paul explains that God "highly exalted him" (2:9), and that all will bend the knee and confess "in heaven and one earth and under the earth" (2:10), and then he was given the title "Lord" (v. 11). Jews used the Greek word here, *kyrios*, to translate the word YHWH, the name of God. In the Greek translation of the Hebrew Scriptures, the Septuagint (c. 250 B.C.), YHWH is translated *kyrios* 90% of the time! In the New Testament, in the context of salvation (such as Philippians 2), *kyrios* is only used of Jesus. In fact, the early church used the term so exclusively of Jesus that when Roman emperors demanded the title Kyrios for themselves, Christians refused to comply. How is Christ's lordship, divinity, humanity, and humble servanthood connected? Cyril of Alexandria (early 5th century A.D.), wrote, "He [Christ] became like us that we might become like him. The work of the Spirit seeks to transform us by grace into a perfect copy of his humbling."[41]

Serve Like Christ (2:12-13)

Paul reminds his intended message to the leaders at Philippi that Christ's service should motivate and stimulate the Philippians to service. He is not physically present with them to offer encouragement, but they do not serve alone! God's activity should minimize their fear (soul) and trembling (body). When he writes, "Work out your own salvation with fear and trembling," he used the word *katergazesthai* (*work out*), conveying the idea of a progression, a bringing to fruition or completion.[42] He is not suggesting a salvation by works, which is contrary to Paul's teaching elsewhere (especially Romans, Galatians, Ephesians 2:1-10, and Titus 3:3-7). Rather, he reminds them that they are saved, but now they have to show it. Not relying on completed or past service, but continued commitment to be a servant leader. This is perhaps what James intended in James 2:18, "Show me your faith apart from your works, and I will show you my faith by my works."

Why should we work with such diligence? What is the spiritual connection it brings? ". . . [F]or it is God who works in you, both to will and to work for his good pleasure" (v. 13). It is not about *your* works, but God's work in you as you commit yourself to serve Him and His people; maturing your faith and life as you minister to others. What better message for a leader: Let God work in and through you!

Christian Distinction (2:14-18)

What is one distinguishing mark of a Christian leader and community? We get along (v. 14)! Paul admonishes them not to become grumblers when called upon to serve, or not try to argue their way out of the opportunity, which seems to be the default of worldly people. He chose two loaded terms to emphasize this point. Expressing his displeasure for those who promote disunity, Paul used the same word that was used in the Greek Old Testament (*göggusmos*) to describe what Israel did to Moses. He also uses *dialogismos* (disputing), signifying an outward, open argument, and in context, an intellectual rebellion against God. Candidly, grumbling and arguing are like two sides to the same coin, feeding from one another (Ex. 16:7-12; Num.14:2, 26, 17:5-25). In v. 14 he may be indicating that the grumbling is against their leaders, just as the Israelites, due to the unexpected suffering they encountered, grumbled against their leaders during the exodus.[43] Paul wants the Philippians to understand their grumbling is not just about leaders or their current situation, but ultimately is grumbling against God Himself!

Paul continues his commentary on grumblers/disputers by describing those of the same mind, the servant leaders of the church, in a distinct manner. In regard to the Philippians and their leaders, Thomas Moore says:

> In this he has provided a model for believers – a model of humble service to benefit others, rather than selfishly hanging on to what they might possess. This willingness to forego status and privilege would have been unheard of among the gods and great leaders known to the Philippians (e.g., Apollo, Zeus, Alexander the Great, the Roman Caesars).[44]

Paul presents a series of metaphors, images that identify and illustrate the Christian distinction as believers but more so as leaders. Verse 15 juxtaposes being a child of God (15a) against being like the present generation (15b). He describes believers as children who are blameless, innocent, without blemish, which may be reminiscent to the sacrificial system, that is, a sacrifice without blemish. Such a child would stand out in comparison to their worldly context, a "crooked and twisted generation."

What is our responsibility to a lost generation? Paul describes us as lights in the darkness, contrasting the brightness of the believer against the darkness of this present generation. He portrays the Christians of Philippi as stars, their brightness as distinct from their darkened context. Similarly, centuries earlier, Daniel wrote that, "those who are wise shall shine like the brightness of the sky above, and those who turn many to righteousness, like the stars forever and ever" (Dan. 12:3). No one can be literally perfect, but in comparison to worldly grumblers, we shine! Chrysostom wrote, "For the stars too shine in darkness yet suffer no diminution of their own beauty, but instead they shine all the brighter."[45]

Paul continues with an athletic image. He tells the Philippians that their conduct, living in accordance with the "word of life" (v. 16) will make him proud. Not only that, it would enable the believers in Philippi to be an example to a lost generation. If we do that, we do not run or labor in vain. The verbiage here speaks of unimpeded running, that one who is either centered on his own interests or is focused on works would impede running; giving rise to self-centeredness and petulant conversations, in a word, grumbling. But the believer who is following Christ does not suffer from such impediments. This introduces another illustration, which will be explored later in 3:12-16. Paul would have been familiar with athletic competitions, given his time in Corinth, home to the Isthmian Games, and the Pan-Ionian games held in Ephesus. His frequent use of athletic illustrations shows that.

Paul's final metaphor in this section reflects on his self-denial. He describes his life and work as a full ritual sacrifice (2:17-18), imagery that is reflects the full process of sacrifice in Numbers 28:1-7.[46] In the passage, he identifies the sacrifice itself (*thysia*), the appropriate ritual (*leitourgia*) involved in the sacrifice, and that his life served the purpose of a drink offering (*spendō*). Decades later, he would use similar imagery in 2 Timothy 4:6, making reference to becoming a drink offering. What's the point? As a sacrifice, he is not boasting in his works, but as a sign of fulfilling God's designated mission. This will become a pivotal point when he addresses the conflict between Euodia and Syntyche (4:2-3), reminding them it's not about them, but to focus on Christ.

Allen says that Philippians 2:12-18 is an allusion to the Old Testament, specifically Deuteronomy and the story of Moses. However, where Moses failed, "Paul expects [the Philippians] to 'succeed.'"[47] But, only if we can keep the same mind and avoid grumbling!

INSIGHTS FROM THE TEXT

Throughout the passage, the leader's connection to Jesus is exemplified and emphasized. Leaders who center their ministry on Christ, having the same mind with both him as well as other mature leaders, are distinct from grumblers, who do not have the same mindedness, neither with one another nor with Christ. As overseers and deacons, we can have the mind of Christ as we serve in one accord, united in purpose.

Leaders Emulate Christ. Christ is not *an* example to imitate, he is *the* example. Paul exemplifies Christ in his own life and ministry. Later in this letter he will hold up Timothy and Epaphroditus as two of those who have followed Christ's example and Paul's pursuit of Christlikeness. Where did Timothy and Epaphroditus learn this? From Paul's example! How do you train future leaders? *Emulation.* This is not only our personal desire to continually grow closer to Christ, but to see those whom we influence grow closer to Christ as well, and even exceed our own ministry. As such, we are *all* living examples of a Christian leader for those who are potential leaders in the church. Jesus, *not us*, becomes the model to emulate. As Paul urged the Corinthians, "Be imitators of me, *as I am of Christ*" (1 Cor. 11:1). Why is Jesus our model? Not only because of who he is (Phil. 2:5-8), but because his example gives us a unique posture in leadership. Leighton Ford wrote, "With Jesus, it is not as easy to separate power and authority. For in him, both are intertwined in the most impressive strength of character."[48] What does all this teach us? What is the message Paul has for leaders? It's *not* about *you*. *Someone* is bigger than your interests. Become more like Him!

Leaders Prioritize Others. In a phrase, this is servant-leadership. Leaders are identified as *servants* (1:1). Paul has already done this, in Philippians as well as in other epistles, as do Peter (2 Peter 1:1) and James (1:1). Cohick reminds us that this is not a call to *contemporary* servant leadership, which is usually voiced in a business or corporate context in regard to institutional growth, but one exemplified by Christ and demonstrated by Paul.[49]

The biblical model of leadership is one that consistently reflects servanthood. The court counselors told newly anointed King Rehoboam, "If you will be a *servant* to this people today and *serve* them, and speak good words to them when you answer them, then they will be your servants forever" (1 Kings 12:7). Centuries later Jesus would instruct the Twelve, "If anyone would be first, he must be last of all and *servant* of all" (Mark 9:33). One chapter later, Jesus offers further instruction to correct their perception of leadership:

> You know that those who are considered rulers of the Gentiles lord it over them, and their great ones exercise authority over them. *But it shall not be so among you.* But whoever would be great among you must be your *servant*, and whoever would be first among you must be *slave* of all. For even the Son of Man came not to be served but *to serve*, and to give his life as a ransom for many (Mark 10:42-45).

This represents a radical change from the world's paradigm of leadership (Figure 4.2)! The "Gentile" model is one with which we are all too familiar, with the leader ultimately benefiting from the labors and service of the followers.

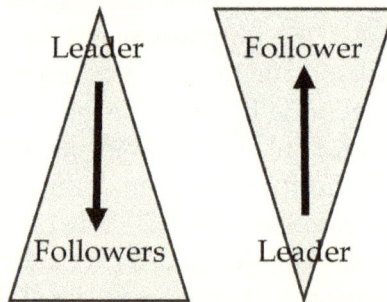

Figure 4.2

However, the biblical model that is centered on Christ, operates under the principle of servanthood. It prioritizes people as ministry, not the means of personal accomplishment. It changes the self-centeredness of the "Gentile" model for Christ-centeredness. Paul would further exemplify this servant posture of leadership in his dealings with the Corinthians. His imagery of ministry in 1 Corinthians 4:1-2, 6-13; reminds them that Christian leadership is not about position or title, but humble Christlike service. Richard

Swartley says that the unity that makes Paul's joy complete (2:2) is due in part to effective leadership, which relies on leaders who have Christlike humility and prioritize others over themselves.[50]

Leaders Make Sacrificial Decisions. Paul describes leaders as selfless, Christ-centered servants. It should be no surprise that he would expect the decision of those leaders to be sacrificial, not self-serving. Referring to Philippians 2:3-4, Swartley says, "Setting aside self-interest to achieve collective decisions, each man carefully monitoring his pride, and checking his opinions lest they have become unquestioned assertions."[51] It is inevitable that we insert ourselves into the decisions we make. It may reflect our unfounded assumptions, personal sentiments, or unique perspective, whether they are right or wrong. If this is done *unintentionally*, that is understandable. Serving alongside other leaders, whether elders or deacons, will probably expose the accidental biased decision. However, what if it is done *intentionally*? What if the driving force behind my decisions as a leader are an individual agenda, self-promotion or for personal benefit? Paul says to us that leaders in God's Kingdom do not lead in this manner. Overseers and deacons lead from a posture of servanthood, reflected in their sacrificial decision making.

Leaders Promote Genuine Unity. When Paul describes the unity, he desires that the Philippian congregation and its leaders emphasize the ideal of same-mindedness. He is essentially advocating for the leadership to be on the proverbial *same page*. He is not being excessive, asking them not to think, or to group-think, or have a hive-mind. He is obviously opposed to grumbling, those who cannot seem to ever get on the same page. He is advocating genuine unity for all the leaders to be united in their servant posture, sacrificial decision making, and same-mindedness following the example of Jesus Christ.

In general, unity can be gained by two forces. The first is external pressure pressing us together (Figure 4.3a). Consider that during World War II the major Allied powers were the United States, Great Britain, and the Soviet Union. Even though their unity was often strained, they managed to stay together due to their common enemies, the Axis Powers. But what happened after the war was won? The external pressure that forged their unity was gone, and the Allies soon became cold war enemies for the next five decades. The unity was forced, never genuine, and so it was also temporary (Figure 4.3a).

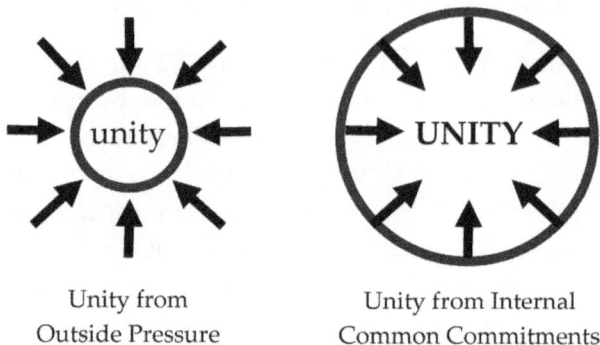

Unity from	Unity from Internal
Outside Pressure	Common Commitments

Figure 4.3

However, if unity is facilitated by internal forces, such as those described previously as same-mindedness, then unity is maintained in spite of the circumstances or external forces (Figure 4.3b). Unity is a genuine quality of the community, one that will last into eternity. When a leadership team is unified, has genuine unity within and between the overseers and deacons, then the potential for unity in the church is greatly enhanced. However, when the opposite is true, when the leadership is everything but a team, is divided and in disarray, the congregation will likewise reflect the disunity present in its leadership. Paul encourages the Philippian leaders to have a leadership team based on internal qualities, Christ-centered same-mindedness, not merely temporary situations, so as to provide servant leadership to the congregation.

Leaders Manage "Grumblers." It would be easy to just avoid grumblers and let them keep grumbling. Please realize that grumbling and conflict are related but are two different items. Conflict tends to be *overt*. Two leaders disagree with one another. A member of the congregation who openly opposes a decision of the overseers. A deacon who takes exception to a decision of the overseers. However, grumbling is usually far less direct, more *covert*. It's the low tone of negativity that seems to permeate every conversation or comment a person or group of people seem to make. It's the passive-aggressive attitude, the quiet comment made to others after a meeting. It's the negative comment made under their breath or demonstrated in their posture. *Deal with the grumblers!* Exercise a measure of compassion, approaching it privately and through conversation, but Paul would have leaders not overlook or avoid such situations. Unchecked grumblers can lead to open conflict! Rather, he would encourage us to engage them constructively through both word and example, reminding them that there is something and Someone more important than them and their self-interests.

PERSONAL & TEAM REFLECTION

1. Identify three ways you exemplify Christ to those around you, especially potential leaders.

2. How unified is your leadership team? Not the mere absence of conflict, but joint movement on the mission of the church (same-mindedness)?

3. What is one way you could better exhibit servant leadership and sacrificial decision making as a leader?

4. Honestly, we can all grumble, occasionally, but not become grumblers. What was the last items you "grumbled" about? Why? How did you overcome your own grumbling?

5. What do the following verses say about grumbling? What should we as leaders do about it?

   - James 5:9
   - 1 Peter 4:9
   - Ephesians 4:29
   - 1 Timothy 2:8
   - John 6:59-71

Chapter 5

Others First vs. Self-Interest (2:19-30)

After tic-tac-toe and checkers, chess is the next level at learning strategy. Most schools and communities have some form of chess club. In the original *Star Trek* (1966) Mr. Spock introduced the world to 23rd century three-dimensional chess.

The game originated in 6th century A.D. India, as a game known as *chaturanga*, as a two-player war game. From India, chess spread to the Middle East and eventually made its way to Europe, where the game was adapted to the European royal courts, and became the modern version of chess. From Europe, it crossed the Atlantic to the Western Hemisphere and children and adults now play it in the United States.

I recently learned that I share a common interest in chess with the president of Dallas Theological Seminary, Dr. Mark Yarborough. He used chess in a chapel message to draw attention to a crucial point of Christian leadership: not all chess pieces are alike. There are pawns, castles (rooks), knights, bishops, and of course the Queen. Each of these pieces has its own range of movement and pattern to follow. Each starts the game in a designated position. Each piece plays a different role and has a different significance in the game. But what if a pawn wanted to be a bishop, or a knight wanted to be a castle? They would undervalue their role and potentially lose the game.

Each piece is crucial. A pawn may win the game or manage to become the Queen under the right circumstances. All pieces know their place, their moves, their limitations, and their roles in the game. However, *most importantly*, they all have *one* common purpose. That they all serve the *King*. Without the King, these pieces are pointless. With the King, they all serve a significant part in the overall strategy.

Paul continues his previous call to servant leadership in this passage. He continues to issue a call to sacrifice for others and the Kingdom as opposed to the self-centered motives of his opponents. He reminds them that we all serve Jesus Christ, and with that servant's posture we are positioned to serve others, to prioritize their needs above our own (2:21-22). While this is applicable to all believers in Jesus, how much more crucial is it for leaders in the church to posture themselves as servants? As overseers and deacons, do we realize our role as servant leaders, in service to the King and the congregation, or do we elevate ourselves to a loftier height than Christ intended for us? Yes, lead like Jesus Christ did, but do we have living examples to follow?

THE TEXT

Philippians 2:19-30 19 I hope in the Lord Jesus to send Timothy to you soon, so that I too may be cheered by news of you. 20 For I have no one like him, who will be genuinely concerned for your welfare. 21 They all seek their own interests, not those of Jesus Christ. 22 But you know Timothy's proven worth, how as a son with a father he has served with me in the gospel. 23 I hope therefore to send him just as soon as I see how it will go with me, 24 and I trust in the Lord that shortly I myself will come also.

25 I have thought it necessary to send to you Epaphroditus my brother and fellow worker and fellow soldier, and your messenger and minister [*leitourgos*] to my need, 26 for he has been longing for you all and has been distressed [*adāmonōn*] because you heard that he was ill. 27 Indeed he was ill, near to death. But God had mercy on him, and not only on him but on me also, lest I should have sorrow upon sorrow. 28 I am the more eager to send him, therefore, that you may rejoice at seeing him again, and that I may be less anxious. 29 So receive him in the Lord with all joy, and honor such men, 30 for he nearly died for the work of Christ, risking [*parabolensamenos*] his life to complete what was lacking in your service to me.

TEXT QUESTIONS

• What does Paul's relationship with Timothy (2:19-22) reveal about the importance of mentorship and companionship in ministry, and how can we apply this to our own relationships?
• How does Paul describe Timothy's character and his relationship to the Philippians in 2:20-22?
• What reason does Paul give for sending Epaphroditus back to the Philippians in 2:25-26?
• How does the example of Epaphroditus (2:25-30) challenge our understanding of service and sacrifice within the church, and what leadership lessons can we learn from his dedication?
• Paul mentions risk and hardship in serving the gospel (v. 30). What implications does that have for how we approach challenges in our leadership situations?
• How does Paul instruct the Philippians to receive Epaphroditus in 2:29, and why does he say they should honor him?

INTO THE TEXT

As previously mentioned, Paul continues his theme from Philippians 2. In the context of exploring the depth of Christ' servanthood, he now reminds the Philippians of two Christlike servant leaders, two men who have been partners with him in the gospel, just as he has urged the Philippians to be also (1:3-18): Timothy and Epaphroditus.

Interestingly, Paul suddenly provides some details of his future travel itinerary. While this is not uncommon for Paul to provide, it usually occurs at the *end* of Paul's letters, such as Colossians 4:7-9, but has occurred in the center (1 Cor. 4:1-19). Why is it located here, in this passage, in Philippians? Why is it important to the point he is making? Don't think like a 21ˢᵗ century traveler. Paul had to let congregations know travel plans and with whom he would be traveling so as to facilitate communication and correspondence. Paul shares his own itinerary in light of the travel exploits of Timothy and Epaphroditus as they hope to serve the Philippians with Paul.

Timothy (2:19-24)

What kind of leader should be emulated? Yes, Christ, but how? Do it as Timothy does it. Timothy is with Paul (v. 19), as the reader would know from the salutation (1:1). In fact, he has been with Paul during Paul's second missionary journey. In Acts, Timothy joins Paul and Silas before they head to Macedonia (Acts 16:1–15) but is curiously absent from the account of Paul in Philippi, including Paul's imprisonment with Silas, and Silas in Thessalonica (17:1–9) and brief engagement at Berea (17:13). The only possibility of his presence with Paul in Philippi would be if he is one of the "we" in Acts 16:7. However, it is not believed that Timothy was imprisoned with Paul and Silas.[52] Timothy then reappears in the Acts narrative when Paul alone is sent on to Athens (17:14–15). Needless to say, Timothy was probably with Paul when he entered Philippi and after he departed the city and would have been readily recognized by the Philippian believers and their leaders ("but you know Timothy's proven worth," v. 22). Why is this important?

Paul juxtaposes the example of Timothy with the behaviors of his opponents. Paul explains the uniqueness of Timothy (v. 20) because he prioritizes those he serves. He prioritizes Jesus Christ, and serving him means serving others, not his own self-interest (v. 21). His opponents, on the other hand, are described as seeking "their own interest" (v. 21a). Paul urges the Philippians and their leaders to essentially remove self-interest, selfishness from their leadership and become selfless.

He continues to extol Timothy, calling him a "son" (v. 22). Paul does this in other letters, highlighting his close relationship with one whom he has known and will know for decades (1 Cor. 4:17; 1 Tim. 1:2, 18; 2 Tim. 1:2). Timothy is a son not merely because of friendship, but because they have served together in advancing the gospel (v. 22). His description of Timothy as his son has a natural order of submission, father-to-son, leader-to-follower; yet he describes Timothy in v. 22 as serving "with me in the gospel," meaning they are *co-servants*, serving together.

Paul uses familial titles to describe many of his co-laborers. Timothy is a son (2:22), and Epaphroditus (2:25) is a brother. Don't overemphasize the distinction between son and brother, since Paul regards Philemon both a partner (Phlm. 17) and child (Phlm. 10). Perhaps these terms indicate a *formative* relationship that Paul and these co-laborers shared. Paul may be saying he is their senior in authority or responsibility, that is, assuming the role of a spiritual father or older brother.

As previously noted, Timothy is with Paul in Rome, but when will he arrive in Philippi? Verses 23-24 indicate Paul is awaiting his verdict in his appeal to Caesar in Acts 25-28. Paul may send Timothy ahead of him as he waits for his release to be finalized.

Epaphroditus (2:25-30)

Epaphroditus is perhaps less familiar than Timothy, but equally important in the Philippian letter. Unlike Timothy, Epaphroditus is only mentioned in Paul's letter to the Philippians, so nothing is known about him other than what's in these few verses and the passing mention in 4:16. His relationship to Paul is extolled by titles such as brother, fellow worker, and fellow soldier. The Philippians sent him to keep Paul informed of the congregation ("your messenger," v. 25), but he also ministered to Paul in his incarceration. The term *leitourgos* is a familiar term in the New Testament, and usually translated *minister* (v. 25). It was indeed used to describe public or civil servants in the ancient world, much like in Great Britain they speak of the "Ministry of" something rather than the "Department of" something and it is led by a minister, e.g. the Prime Minister. Paul explains that in his hour of need, the Philippians provided someone to minister to him on their behalf.

Epaphroditus had his own reasons for leaving Paul in Rome (2:26-27), but Paul expounds even more (2:28-30). Paul has *sent* Epaphroditus home to Philippi due to a personal reason: he was a bit "homesick" (v. 26). As in English, one can describe "distress" with a variety of terms that indicate the intensity of the condition. Here, Paul uses *adāmonōn* (v. 26), implying that it occupied his mind to the point of distraction, confusion and even physical ailment, which he also seems to have encountered. Paul further explains that Epaphroditus' illness was not mild, but "near to death" (v. 27), once again affirming the value of Epaphroditus to him personally and as a co-laborer in the gospel, expressing that his death would have brought "sorrow upon sorrow" (v. 27). No indication is given as to the nature of his illness, other than the severity of it; but it was enough to mention to those who sent him.

Paul is providing a justification for Epaphroditus' return home, perhaps sooner than the Philippians expected. His illness was obviously a concern for Paul as well as the Philippians, and he explains that his arrival home will both benefit the Philippians and relieve Paul's own anxiety in the matter (v. 28). Essentially, Epaphroditus will carry news of Paul as well as this letter to the Philippians and their leaders, and Paul will be better able to focus on his ministry without Epaphroditus' health condition distracting him. This should not be interpreted as a detriment to Epaphroditus, given Paul's earlier high praise, but also the honor afforded him in verse 30.

He instructs the Philippian congregation and their leaders who sent Epaphroditus to "receive him . . . and honor such men." Paul wants to ensure that Epaphroditus' return is not due to failure or detrimental service, but because he had fulfilled his commission even to the point of death. Paul uses the term *parabolensamenos*, *risk*, in verse 30 which literally means to gamble; these were leaders were willing to gamble their lives for the sake of the Kingdom of God. The Philippian leaders sent Epaphroditus to fulfill a mission of supporting Paul during his Roman incarceration, and having fulfilled this, Paul now sends him home with high praise and regard. Theodoret (AD 393-457) erroneously suggests that Epaphroditus held a position *superior* to that of the elders, making them his *subordinates*. However, there is absolutely no evidence for this in the text nor historically.[53] Hence, Epaphroditus may have been an elder or deacon in the church, but we don't know for sure.

It should be noted that Paul makes one additional reference to Epaphroditus in this epistle. Once again, it is in praise of the Philippians and specifically Epaphroditus. In a Roman prison, even home confinement, family and friends were expected to provide the prisoners' needs. Paul explains that Epaphroditus delivered the gift from the Philippians, a gift that was "received in full, and more. I am well supplied . . ." (4:18-19). Epaphroditus was indeed a minister, a servant leader, like Christ, like Paul, like Timothy, putting the needs of others, especially Paul, before his own self-interests.

INSIGHTS FROM THE TEXT

Leaders Learn From Leaders. Having given the example of Jesus as servant leader in Philippians 2, why does he now present them with the examples of Timothy and Epaphroditus? Isn't Jesus enough? Paul later explains, "Brothers, join in imitating me, and keep your eyes on those who walk according to the example you have in us [presumably him and Timothy, 1:1]" (Philippians 3:17). While there are more ways to learn leadership, following the example of others as they follow Christ is perhaps the most natural. More formal means are always beneficial, such as reading books or participating in conferences, and these have their value; but having someone to serve as a mentor, an example, has far more impact than mere reading a book or hearing a speaker. Personally, I've had the privilege of hearing phenomenal preaching and teaching throughout my life, I enjoy reading a book per week, and I spend regular time with peers. But, in reflection, I have been blessed to have leaders who took the time to pour into my life, to spend time to answer questions, to encourage me when I failed, share coffee and conversation, and to advise me even when I didn't want it. They had a more profound influence on me. Yes, some of them were pastors and professors, but it was the time *beyond* the worship service or classroom that I remember the most.

We all have someone who has poured into our lives. It may have been a parent, a teacher, a relative, or in this instance, perhaps a leader at church who exemplified what it meant to be an elder or deacon. Paul says it is essential to follow godly models of faith and service in order to grow in Christ as a believer and a leader. Dr. Howard Hendricks of Dallas Theological Seminary, a leader and educator, used to ask his students a simple and yet profound question, "Who is your Paul? Who is your Timothy?" Who is mentoring, coaching, discipling you? For whom are you doing all this? Paul gives us the example of Timothy and Epaphroditus for a reason, and this is it!

Leadership is Collaborative. We have noted since the first verse of Philippians that the church's leadership is plural, with no single leader other than Jesus Christ (Acts 4:11; Col. 1:18-20; Eph. 5:22-25). Overseers/elders and deacons are plural. However, this takes it one step further. It's not just about the *quantity* of the leadership team, but the *quality* of the leadership team. Paul and Timothy served together as spiritual father-and-son. Paul and Epaphroditus were co-workers in Christ, soldiering for the gospel. They worked together as a *team.*

The dynamics that govern a team are somewhat simple, but difficult to balance. First, the team's purpose is the personal priority of every participant. This means that individual agendas, self-interests, and personal preferences are sacrificed for the greater purpose of the team, just as Paul described Timothy as one who prioritized the interests and needs of others and not himself (2:20). The second dynamic in a team is the relationship shared by the team members. Not necessarily on a personal basis, but a recognition of the contribution each member of the team brings to the table. It is a sense of *synergy* that we accomplish more together than working separately. Acknowledging we all have a role and place on the team ultimately contributes to its success. Once again, notice how Paul describes Timothy, and also Epaphroditus: their contribution to his ministry added immeasurably to it. Paul could have accomplished much on his own, but realized even more could be achieved with a team.[54] This principle is captured in the sentiments often attributed to the late President Ronald Reagan, "There is no limit to the amount of good you can do if you don't care who gets the credit."[55]

Leaders Grant Honor. Just because leaders assume the posture of servant, perform service in the interest of others, and even sacrifice for the sake of the church *doesn't* mean they are *not* due some recognition. You should affirm them as servant leaders! Paul offers honor to Timothy and Epaphroditus in this passage in recognition of their service to his ministry and to the church. In fact, Fee suggests that this portion of Philippians reads like a letter of commendation, as if Paul were providing a reference for Timothy and Epaphroditus.[56] Servant leaders rarely if ever extol their *own* accomplishments, nor do they assess their level of sacrifice. To do so would perhaps lead them to question their genuineness. Hence, it is crucial that others offer the honor on their behalf, in recognition of those things they would never extol for themselves.

When Paul describes what a "living sacrifice" looks like, he writes, "Love one another with brotherly affection. *Outdo* one another in showing *honor*" (Rom. 12:10). Leaders should seek to form a culture of gratitude and thankfulness within the congregation. An ethos where recognition is given to individuals who serve with distinction and serve as examples for others to follow, encouraging them to volunteer, utilize their gifts, and serve.

On a personal note, my father, James Sr., enjoyed serving as a deacon in our home church. My father was humble. He never graduated from high school, but owned his own paint-contracting business, and was always supportive of my calling. Three momentos hung on the wall behind his recliner, where he sat most nights after a long day on a project: his framed certificate from the "Kentucky Colonels," from his home state, a large big-mouth bass he caught in Herrington Lake, and one more item, a plaque from our home church thanking him for the service he provided during a building campaign. He was proud to have served, and thankful for the acknowledgement.

Leaders Recognize Differences. One of the first lessons in ministry is to realize not everyone is like you. Timothy realized this principle and was described as one "who will be genuine concerned for your welfare," as opposed to those who "seek their own interests, not those of Jesus Christ" (2:20). We are more capable of ministry when we realize that we are not in ministry to ourselves but to others. When we fail to recognize differences, ministry opportunities pass unnoticed and unrecognized. Servant leaders can value the differences in people, but Paul's opponents fail to do so.

Becoming aware of our congregation, their individual needs as well as the corporate needs, allows us to minister to those within the congregation. However, also knowing the needs of those who are in our community, our neighborhood, widens our outreach. We are more capable of connecting with those who are outside of Christ, demonstrating the love of Jesus to those who have not yet accepted him, evangelizing. To do this, we need to recognize their genuine needs by removing the filter of our self-interests.

PERSONAL & TEAM REFLECTION

1. How do you keep your own interests, *self*, in check?

2. How do you respond when you don't get "your way"? What curbs or tempers your response?

3. How have or can you put the needs of another in front of your own needs? How does this impact how your church does ministry?

4. How does your congregation demonstrate honor? How does it show gratitude in recognition to those who serve in the church?

5. To quote Howard Hendricks, "Who is your Paul? Who is your Timothy?" Identify each of them in your life and share the positive influence your "Paul" has had and continues to have on you.

Chapter 6

Christ-Confidence vs. Self-Confidence (3:1-11)

I have had opportunity to serve on *way too many* search teams. Search teams for church staff members, for the lead pastor position, for professors and academic staff positions, even for college presidential positions. I would not care to guess the number of résumés and *curriculum vitae* I've waded through over the 40 years of ministry. A résumé can only take a search team so far, then comes the interview.

I have learned a substantial amount of wisdom and insight from others about how to conduct interviews and how to assess an interviewee. Perhaps the best piece of advice I ever heard, and one that I still use today, is to listen for "God-talk." No, not listening for God to speak to the search team. Rather, as a candidate is being interviewed, does the candidate ever naturally, in the course of dialog, use God language? Perhaps when you highlight one of their achievements, they reply, "the Lord really opened a door for that to happen . . . ," or when giving them a compliment regarding their leadership, "God brought a team together better than I could have done intentionally. . . ." Not self-deprecating, not a fake humility, but acknowledging that God was active in their ministry and leadership. Affirming a personal dependence upon the Lord even as a leader. Imagine the opposite! You make these comments and observations to a candidate and hear in response, "Yes, *I am* quite accomplished, *I've* done a great deal, you'd be fortunate to have *me*. . . ." "Why yes, *my team*, that *I led*, performed admirably under *my* direction. . . ."

Continuing to build on the theme of servant leadership, Paul warns them again about a group of false teachers who offer a different gospel, one that does not wholly rely on Christ for their salvation and new life. Their teaching results in an overemphasis on self-centered confidence, based on personal achievement and stature, as opposed to Christ-centered confidence, focusing on the finished work of Jesus

Christ and the new life found in him. Where does your confidence lie? Does your confidence lie in Christ or in yourself? The church needs confident leaders, but based on whom?

THE TEXT

Philippians 3:1-11 1 Finally, my brothers, rejoice in the Lord. To write the same things to you is no trouble to me and is safe for you.

2 Look out for the dogs, look out for the evildoers, look out for those who mutilate [*katatomēn*] the flesh. 3 For we are the real circumcision, who worship by the Spirit of God and glory in Christ Jesus and put no confidence in the flesh— 4 though I myself have reason for confidence in the flesh also. If anyone else thinks he has reason for confidence in the flesh, I have more: 5 circumcised [*peritomē*] on the eighth day, of the people of Israel, of the tribe of Benjamin, a Hebrew of Hebrews; as to the law, a Pharisee; 6 as to zeal, a persecutor of the church; as to righteousness, under the law blameless. 7 But whatever gain I had, I counted as loss for the sake of Christ. 8 Indeed, I count everything as loss because of the surpassing worth of knowing Christ Jesus my Lord. For his sake I have suffered the loss of all things and count them as rubbish [*skubala*], in order that I may gain Christ 9 and be found in him, not having a righteousness of my own that comes from the law, but that which comes through faith in Christ [*dia pisteōs Christou*], the righteousness from God that depends on faith— 10 that I may know him and the power of his resurrection, and may share his sufferings, becoming like him in his death, 11 that by any means possible I may attain the resurrection from the dead.

TEXT QUESTIONS

- In Philippians 3:2, what warning does Paul give to the Philippians, and to whom is he referring?

84

- How does Paul's warning against confidence in the flesh (vv. 2-3) challenge our tendencies to find security in achievements or status, and what does it mean to truly put our confidence in Christ?
- In Philippians 3:7-9, what does Paul consider more valuable than his past accomplishments?
- How can Paul's perspective on considering everything as loss for the sake of Christ (v. 8) motivate us to reevaluate our own priorities and attachments as leaders?
- How does Paul contrast confidence in the flesh with righteousness through faith in Philippians 3:9?
- What is Paul's ultimate desire as expressed in Philippians 3:10-11?
- What does it mean to know Christ and the power of his resurrection (v. 10) and how can we experience this in our daily lives and spiritual practices?

INTO THE TEXT

One of my mentors was the late Wayne B. Smith, founding preacher of Southland Christian Church in Lexington, Kentucky. One weekend in 1981, while he drove me back from college in Cincinnati, I took the occasion to ask him if he had any suggestions for a person preparing to enter the preaching ministry. He said one sentence, "There is no such thing as a bad *short* sermon." While he said this in jest, it has actually proven valuable over the decades since that conversation.

Paul opens this section with "Finally" (3:1), but he is literally only halfway through the letter! However, it is in 3:1-11 that Paul raises the alarm regarding a serious theological threat that has a practical expression for the Philippian leadership. Theologically, the opposition is from those who continue to place confidence in the Law and Judaism, *Judaizers*, as opposed to those who find confidence in the grace of Jesus Christ. Paul appears to make an abrupt pivot from his affirmation of Timothy's and Epaphroditus' faithfulness to Christ to a complete condemnation of Judaism's incursion into the Philippian church. In this instance, his opposition started outside the congregation, from the Jewish community, but is also from within the congregation, those who profess Christ but still require observance of the Mosaic law and the traditions of the elders for salvation and/or spiritual maturity. Facing such external opposition in Philippi is nothing new for Paul.

- "But though we had already *suffered and been shamefully treated at Philippi,* as you know, we had boldness in our God to declare to you the gospel of God in the midst of much conflict" (1 Thes. 2:2-3).

- "They have beaten us publicly, uncondemned, men who are Roman citizens, and have thrown us into prison; and do they now throw us out secretly? No! Let them come themselves and take us out" (Acts 16:37-38).

However, Paul is in fact exploring the theological distinction of Christ-centered servant leadership as opposed to those who do not embrace it, those who have a self-centered posture; like those he opposed previously in Philippians 2.

"Finally"? (3:1)

In all fairness to Paul, when he says "finally" he probably means to indicate the close of his opening remarks, and now is pivoting to address additional matters in his letter. He returns to the familiar and common theme of "rejoice in the Lord." He is writing to them about "the same thing," reminding them that the truth bears repeating. What he is about to share was probably familiar to the Philippians, Paul having taught them, he is simply reminding them of what they should have already known. He says in conclusion that repeating his instruction is "no trouble" and is not done for his own benefit, but out of concern for them, "safe to you." Remember, the truth bears repeating.

Judaizers vs. Genuine Believers (3:2-3)

Put simply, Judaizers were those who insisted that Gentile Christians were required to follow the Mosaic law and the traditions of Judaism even after affirming Christ, and in fact affirm this even prior to accepting Christ as Savior.[57] Paul first encountered this theological issue upon his return to Antioch from the first missionary journey, resulting in the Jerusalem Council (Acts 15). However, he continues to encounter Judaizers throughout his mission, engaging most heavily on the subject in his letter to the Galatians when discussing our freedom in Christ (Galatians 5:1-15). Without a doubt the Judaizers were the most significant theological threat to the church of the first century A.D. What are Paul's sentiments about the Judaizers in Philippi? How does he describe them?

"Dogs . . . evildoers . . . [those who] mutilate the flesh" (3:2). Let's unpack Paul's description. *Dogs* may have been domesticated, but were generally *despised* by the Jews. When used figuratively to describe people, it was "a term of contempt" (1 Sam. 17:43; Matt. 15:26; Mark 7:27), often used to describe Gentiles.[58] Dogs were not pets. Some had been domesticated for rural farm work, but in the cities, dogs had no home or owners. They were just packs of dogs scavenging for food and fighting in the streets. In fact, in Psalms the imagery of a dog was a term applied to one's enemies![59] Paul leaves little to the imagination in his assessment of the Judaizers, using a derogatory image to describe them.

Evildoers seems to be a general statement regarding the results of their message and activities. Judaizers are false teachers, and hence their activity is a detriment to the advancement of the gospel, Paul's mission with the Philippians. Essentially, the Judaizers offer nothing good, nothing of benefit to the Philippians. Given the context of Philippians 2, their interests are their own, with no concern for the spiritual growth or maturity of the congregation.

One key teaching of the Judaizers involved circumcision. As the symbol of the Mosaic covenant, it was what they required for all converts, i.e. requiring Gentile converts to first submit to the Old Testament covenant before accepting Christ. While he mentions *circumcision* in 3:3 and 3:5 (*peritomē*), some maintain that Paul uses a play on words, referring to the Judaizers not as circumcisers, but *mutilators* (*katatomēn*), "those who mutilate the flesh" (3:2). In the following verses Paul will convert the symbol of the Old Covenant into a symbol for spiritual destruction. When Paul wrote the church at Galatia, warning them of the Judaizer heresy, he wrote, "I wish those who unsettle you [those who "preach circumcision"] would emasculate themselves" (Gal. 5:12), possibly referring to the requirements of the Mosaic law in Deuteronomy 23:1, "No one whose testicles are crushed or whose male organ is cut off shall enter the assembly of the Lord." Paul gives no credence, not in Philippians or in Galatians, to the Judaizers, either theologically or practically.

In verse 3 Paul begins to draw the distinction between adamant adherents to the old covenant in the church, the Judaizers, with those of the new covenant, Jews and Gentiles together, Christians. He draws a sharp distinction between those whose confidence is in Christ and his righteousness, versus those whose confidence is in the flesh, their works and self-righteousness. First, Paul refers to Christians as being the real people of God, "we are the circumcision" (v. 3), not them! They may have the physical circumcision of the flesh, but we have the spiritual circumcision of the heart. This is a familiar theme in Paul's writings, such as in his letter to the Colossians, "In him also you were circumcised with a circumcision made without hands, by putting off the body of the flesh, by the circumcision of Christ . . ." (Col. 2:11). Second, because of this, we are those who "worship by the Spirit of God," once again emphasizing the distinction between confidence in the flesh vs confidence in the Spirit. Third, unlike the Judaizers, we "glory in Christ Jesus," rather than in our own achievements, works, and acts of righteousness. Finally, unlike the others, we place "no confidence in the flesh," realizing that it is Jesus in Whom our confidence lies, and not ourselves. Paul is reaffirming what he has written in Ephesians, "For by grace you have been saved through faith. And this is not your own doing; it is the gift of God, not a result of works, so that no one may boast" (Eph. 2:8-9). Truth bears repeating.

Paul's Résumé (3:4-6)

Earlier, the chapter opened with some advice about reviewing résumés and interviewing pastoral candidates. Over the next few verses it is as if Paul were espousing his résumé, his qualifications to be a leader. *Why?* In context, he is pitting himself against the Judaizers. If their criteria are in the flesh, self-righteousness, works of the law, then Paul exclaims that he has reason to possess *more* confidence in the flesh than any of them! Look at the points of his résumé:

Verse	Item	Significance	Message to Judaizers
v. 5	*Ritual*	Fulfilled the requirements of the Covenant (Gen. 17:12; Lev. 12:5)	I am just as much a Hebrew-Jew as you, if not more!
v. 5	*Nationality*	"Of the people of Israel"	I too am part of the people of God's covenant with Abraham and Moses!
v. 5	*State*	Tribe of Benjamin, with a rich heritage (1 Sam. 9:1-2; 1 Kgs. 12:21; Ezra 4:1)	I'm not just an Israelite, but from a highly regarded, historically significant tribe! (Think of it like someone saying, "I'm from Texas!")
v. 5	*Stature*	"A Hebrew of Hebrews"	I'm not the average adherent to Judaism, my faith and life are exemplary.
v. 5	*Sect*	"A Pharisee" (Acts 22:32; 23:6; 26:5)	I was not just a faithful Jew, but a teacher of the Law and Tradition of the Elders.
v. 6	*Activist*	Zealous to the point of persecuting those who opposed Judaism! (Acts 9:1-2)	I didn't try to dialog and convert those who opposed the faith, I literally sought to murder them!
v. 6	*Righteous-ness*	Self-righteous, "blameless" by the Law of Moses	Judaizers, go ahead, try to find fault with me! I can be as self-righteous as any of you!

What's Paul's point? If it is confidence in the flesh you want, Paul's your man. He has it all and then some. Whose résumé could possibly compete? If the Judaizers think they are what God is wanting, Paul is even more! Why does he do this? Paul is setting the Philippians up for his next point.

Does it Really Matter? (3:7-11)

Everything the Judaizers and Paul himself once cherished and prized, he now not only discounts, but regards as loss, not gain (v. 7). He likewise says "I consider" three times in 3:7-8 and "I reckon" in 3:13 regarding his assessment on his circumstances. Paul borrows some specific language from economics to explain the value he places or doesn't place on his worldly achievements when he speaks of "gain" (3:7, 8) and loss (3:8). How does he assess his pre-Christian life and accomplishments under Judaism? What value does it hold now? In 3:8 uses a rather graphic term, *skubala*, rotting garbage or even excrement! Substantially, this is what the Judaizers are promoting! But, all this loss, to gain *what*?

Not a what, a *who*! Paul repeatedly says he has gained Christ! Twice Paul extols the benefits, the gain, of knowing Christ (3:8, 10). Paul explains it all beginning at the close of v. 8, "that I may gain Christ and be found in him, not having a righteousness of my own that comes from the law [which the Judaizers proclaim], but that which comes through faith in Christ, the righteousness from God that depends on faith" (3:8c-9). This is the doctrine of justification! That salvation is not based on my faithfulness, my works, my adherences, my perfection, but on Jesus Christ, who grants his righteousness to us. An intriguing translation issue arises in v. 9 that underscores this point. The phrase *dia pisteōs Christou* can be rendered two ways depending on how certain nuances of Greek syntax is understood. It can emphasize "faith *in* Christ," known as an objective genitive, where Christ is the subject of *our* faith. However, it can also be translated "faith *of* Christ" as what is known as a subjective genitive, which stresses the faithfulness of Christ, *his* faithfulness is the basis of our salvation. Either way, the center, the focal point of our faith is Christ Jesus, in him we place our confidence, and not in ourselves. Paul is proclaiming that, compared to Christ, my résumé is rubbish!

All this results in an amazing transformation of one's life. Salvation, God's justification and sanctification through Jesus Christ, is experienced now and we await our future glorification. Paul explains this as he concludes the section (vv. 10-11). When we know Christ Jesus, we experience the power of his resurrection (v. 10), identifying with Jesus in his struggling and suffering, so that one day we too may be glorified, "becoming like him in his death, that by any means possible I may attain the resurrection of the dead (v. 10c-11). For Paul, to know Christ was not a mere theological exercise in Christology or creedal adherence. Nor was it just an intellectual affirmation of the fact of Jesus' biography. Paul wanted to know Jesus Christ on a personal, intimate level; a subjective knowledge of him, experientially, not just "a brain on a stick" (v. 10-11). It is not automatic or instantaneous; it is a progression of growth in Christ. Figure 6.1 illustrates this *in reverse*, based on Philippians 3:10-11, beginning with the result and going back to its start.

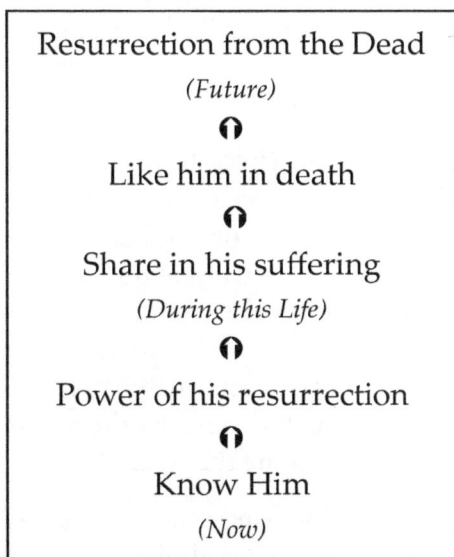

Resurrection from the Dead
(Future)
⋂
Like him in death
⋂
Share in his suffering
(During this Life)
⋂
Power of his resurrection
⋂
Know Him
(Now)

Figure 6.1

For Paul, it all starts with knowing Christ. It is future focused, as we wait for our resurrection with him in the end time, yet our lives are Christ-centered in the past, present, and future. This is why Paul's confidence is not centered on himself, but on Christ Jesus. He will not be swayed by the Judaizers, nor should the believers and leaders at Philippi. The Judaizers cannot and could not offer the promises Christ gives us. Paul's confidence was in Jesus Christ and him crucified, raised, glorified, and our eternal presence with him.

INSIGHTS FROM THE TEXT

Leaders Are Diligent. One qualification that elders and deacons share in common is theological integrity, orthodoxy (1 Tim. 3:9; Titus 1:9-12). Paul opens this section of his letter to the Philippians saying that "to write *the same things* to you is not trouble to me and is safe for you" (3:1), and then proceeds to give a stern warning about the false teachers among them. As elders and deacons in the church we need to be watchful for those whom Paul describes as "dogs" and "evildoers," those whose actions would be contrary to the good health of the Body of Christ. Without diligent leaders, false teaching will always find a way into the church. Paul is urging those in leadership to address this situation, not to let it fester or infect the church any further.

Leaders Don't Avoid Conflict. If you peruse books, websites, and listen to podcasts on conflict management, you become aware of numerous postures and styles of conflict management. One that is almost always used but is equally almost always ineffective and even wrong is simply to *avoid* the conflict and allow the matter to go unresolved, unchecked, tolerated. Eventually leaders who avoid conflict appear to compromise their integrity. The Philippian leaders could have just tolerated the Judaizers, let them have their say, never confront them. Can you imagine the results?

Not avoiding conflict does *not* mean to instigate conflict nor does it mean to be a trip-hammer when dealing with difficult situations, but simply to avoid unpleasant circumstances is ill advised. I have coached churches where a conflict ensued and their approach was, "Just give it no attention, pretend it isn't even here, it will burn out and things will go back to normal." Would you want a firefighter to take this approach? The conflict did eventually burn out, burning about half the congregation, leaving anything but a normal situation. Leadership could have easily addressed matter of the conflict, but rather than engaging, they withdrew from the situation.

Leaders Are Spiritually Qualified. Paul is self-aware. He knows his résumé. He recognizes his own caliber in comparison to that of those in his group, his resume stands out as a "Hebrew of Hebrews." But what qualified him to be a leader among the pharisees and the adherents of Judaism is *not* what qualifies him to lead in God's Kingdom.

While Paul is obviously aware of his worldly qualifications as a leader, his real qualifications are those that have released him from the religion of Judaism for a personal relationship with Christ Jesus. Paul's new "résumé" is his relationship with Jesus and his focus on eschatological reunion with him. Do not misunderstand me. Paul's earthly preparations served him well as an apostle. His knowledge of Scripture and Jewish tradition was a benefit for his ministry, and it was gained with his preparations as a rabbi, "educated at the feet of Gamaliel according to the strict manner of the law of our fathers . . ." (Acts 22:3b). When those serving in church leadership can bring to the table the skills and training received for their careers, it is of immeasurable benefit to the congregation, as long as they are spiritually qualified as well. *As long as* the spiritual qualifications for a leader are not substituted for their business acumen the church will benefit from these leaders. When Paul penned his letters to Timothy and Titus, and described a Christian leader, overseers-elders and deacons, the depiction is one of a spiritually mature follower of Jesus Christ (1 Tim. 3:1-14; Titus 1:5-16). Peter's first epistle would agree, connecting the shepherds to their "chief Shepherd," and describing them as humble servant-leaders (1 Pet. 5:1-5).

There were elders in the last ministry in which I served who held high positions in major corporations, such Georgia Pacific, State Farm, and Chick-fil-a. Their professional experiences gave them insights into church finance, arranging staff searches, providing for staff health, and addressing the inevitable conflicts every church faces. But, more importantly, when they sat around that table, they were no longer corporate leaders, they were the overseers-elders of God's flock. They began each meeting with a meal and an hour of prayer. They delved into Scripture in their decision making. They prioritized their relationship with Christ and one another as a team, over their résumés. (I must admit, the free Chick-fil-a was a much-appreciated bonus!)

Leaders Prioritize Christ. Paul had a lot on his proverbial plate in Philippi and elsewhere. When he tells about all the harm that has befallen him because of his ministry (2 Corinthians 11:21-27), which includes beatings, being lashed, stoned, shipwrecked, and the dangers encountered when traveling long distances, he concludes with "And, apart from other things, there is the daily pressure on me of my anxiety for all the churches" (2 Cor. 11:28). Yet in all matters, he prioritizes his relationship with Jesus Christ as of prime importance.

John C. Maxwell, popular leadership specialist, describes 3:7-14 as "the law of priorities," where Paul "discerned what hindered him (vv. 7-8) . . . discovered what he wanted (vv. 9-11) . . . [and] determined how to get it (vv. 12-14)."[60] Paul simply wanted to know Jesus, now and into eternity. This primacy of knowing Jesus will be further explored in the next chapter, where Paul explains his fixation on Christ as the core of his life.

PERSONAL & TEAM REFLECTION

1. Can you think of occasions where it is easy to slip into a more self-centered confidence posture? When and why?

2. Can you identify one element of your life, an item on your "résumé," that you bring to the table as a leader?

3. How do you ensure that you do not overly depend on your abilities and understanding as a leader rather than those of Christ?

4. If you were writing a spiritual résumé for your life, what would it have on it? What items would identify you as a spiritual leader?

5. Identify one way you can be more Christ-confident than self-confident as a leader in the church.

Chapter 7

Stand vs. Swayed (3:12-21)

If you were alive on August 7, 1954 and had a television set, you probably watched the British Empire and Commonwealth Games in Vancouver, British Columbia, Canada. Why? Earlier that summer, John Landy from Australia and Roger Bannister from England broke the "Four-Minute-Mile" in separate qualifying races, with Landy outpacing Bannister's time by 1.4 seconds! Now they would compete in the same race in front of over 35,000 spectators in the stands, plus worldwide coverage in newspapers, and on radio and television.

The race was promoted as "The Mile of the Century" and later dubbed the "Miracle Mile." As the starting gun was fired and the race began, Landy and Bannister were tight in their lanes with Landy in the lead. *But*, with only 90 yards remaining in the mile run, Landy *turns his head to the left*, looking *back* over his shoulder in hopes of seeing Bannister behind him, taking his eye *off* the goal, which was all the difference Bannister needed to pass him on Landy's *right*! The image has become iconic!

Bannister outpaced Landy by 0.8 seconds for the victory![61] Landy's *faux pas* was witnessed by thousands in the stands, captured in newspapers, and reported on radio and televised around the globe. The incident was so iconic that it has been immortalized in a statue outside the stadium depicting Landy's over-the-shoulder glance to the left. Bannister won because he remained focused on what was ahead and not becoming distracted by what was behind or beside him.

Paul employs the imagery of a race, among other illustrations, to encourage the church at Philippi, and especially their leaders. In the latter part of Philippians 3, he urges their leaders to stand firm in their ministry, focused on the goal ahead of them, who is Christ Jesus; rather than being swayed, losing sight of the goal and moving ministry off course, compromising. Will we be leaders who remain forward-focused in our ministry or become easily swayed by distractions?

THE TEXT

Philippians 3:12–4:1 12 Not that I have already obtained this or am already perfect, but I press on to make it my own, because Christ Jesus has made me his own. 13 Brothers, I do not consider that I have made it my own. But one thing I do: forgetting what lies behind and straining forward to what lies ahead, 14 I press on toward the goal for the prize of the upward call of God in Christ Jesus. 15 Let those of us who are mature [*teleios*] think this way, and if in anything you think otherwise, God will reveal that also to you. 16 Only let us hold true [*stoichein*] to what we have attained.

17 Brothers, join in imitating me, and keep your eyes on those who walk according to the example you have in us. 18 For many, of whom I have often told you and now tell you even with tears, walk as enemies of the cross of Christ. 19 Their end is destruction, their god is their belly, and they glory in their shame, with minds set on earthly things. 20 But our citizenship [*politeuma*] is in heaven, and from it we await a Savior, the Lord Jesus Christ, 21 who will transform [*metaschāmatisei*] our lowly body to be like his glorious body, by the power [*dunamis*] that enables him even to subject all things to himself.

4:1 Therefore, my brothers, whom I love and long for, my joy and crown, stand firm thus in the Lord, my beloved.

TEXT QUESTIONS

- What does Paul admit about his own spiritual journey in Philippians 3:12, and how does he describe his pursuit of it?
- In Philippians 3:13-14, what does Paul say he does in his efforts to reach his goal?

- What does Paul urge mature believers, such as leaders, to do in Philippians 3:15, and what does he suggest will happen if they think differently?
- What does it mean to "press on" toward the goal for the prize of the heavenly call of God in Christ Jesus in v. 14? How can this focus shape our decisions and actions as leaders?
- In what ways can the call to have the same mind and attitude as Paul (v. 15) inspire us to foster unity and humility within our own congregation?
- In Philippians 3:20, where does Paul say the Philippians' citizenship is, and what do believers eagerly await?
- How does Paul's exhortation to "stand firm in the Lord" (Philippians 4:1) reflect the challenges faced by believers, and what practical steps can we take to remain steadfast in our faith?

INTO THE TEXT

As mentioned previously, Paul was familiar with athletic competitions, and employed the imagery of games throughout his writings (for example, 1 Cor. 9:24-27; 1 Tim. 4:7-8; 2 Tim. 2:5, 4:6-8). Once again, he uses the imagery of a track race to depict the Christian life, and to encourage the Philippian leaders to stay focused, take a stand, and not be swayed off course.

Race of Faith (3:12-16)

Continuing his thought from the previous section, Paul says his life objective to "attain the resurrection from the dead" (3:15) is still the same, but is not yet a reality in his life. This becomes the single-minded focus of his life. It is something towards which he continues to make progress, but has not yet attained. His race is one of living out Christ in his life (v. 12). Remember his comment about "Work out your salvation" (2:12)? This is exactly what he is exemplifying here. Paul's motivation is not in himself, not a focus on the self, but he presses on "because Christ Jesus has made me his own" (v. 12). How?

First, by not placing faith in himself (v. 13a). It's not about him, it's all about Christ in him, living out Christ in his life. Second, he continues *facing forward* toward Jesus Christ (v. 13b). It is difficult to imagine trying to make progress while looking backwards. Third, releasing the past's hold on him allows him to strain forward. We have all seen the Olympic track competitions as they approach the last lap, the final leg of their race. With the goal in sight, they push their bodies forward to be the first one to contact the ribbon. This is what Paul is doing. Notice the process of change indicated here. One focuses on the attainable goal, releasing anything that may impede your progress, and then pouring all you have into reaching "what lies ahead" (v. 13c). It would be easy for a leader to forget to be a Christian and lean on their own understanding and agenda, but in v. 13 Paul counsels against it on the spiritual basis that we are all centered on Christ. Paul doesn't target his own growth, benefit, or achievement; but rather the cross. To conclude this thought, he describes his goal, the objective he pursues and strains forward to reach. The goal and prize is the call of Jesus Christ on his life.

Paul now turns his attention from his example toward those who are "mature," which should include the leadership of the Philippian congregation. When he describes them as *mature*, Paul uses the familiar word *teleios*, indicating completion or sometimes perfection, and was often used to describe an adult as opposed to a child.[62] He had previously used a form of this word in v. 12, possibly as a wordplay against his opponents who think of themselves as already perfect. But Paul says he has not yet reached it, but there are those among the Philippians, presumably their leaders, who are like Paul, still maturing.[63] He presents a metaphor of imitation in v. 15, those who are mature will imitate his race, they will "think this way." He doesn't stop there. He addresses the immature, saying if you don't understand what he is saying, if you are *at this time* incapable of running the race he is describing, give yourself some time to mature. God will make sure you are eventually prepared. Once again, he urges them to stay focused on the goal.

Paul's final line in this section has a crucial message to those who race in their relation to Christ. "Only let us hold true to what we have attained" (3:16). Paul chose his terms with intentionality when he used *stoichein*, "hold true." The term implied strict adherence to the path, like marching in the military or following battle orders.[64] In context, it perhaps reflects athletes racing in their own lane, not swaying or drifting into another runner's path. It is more than a reinforcement to keep focused. He reminds them to realize what they have already attained, how far they have already come, but with a cloaked warning to not become complacent. Do not stop now just because you have attained so much. Keep running! As we mature in Christ, we become more aware of entanglements, hindrances to our faith. The author of Hebrews, possibly Paul, penned a similar caution, "Therefore, since we are surrounded by so great a cloud of witnesses, let us also lay aside *every weight*, and *sin* which clings so closely, and let us run *with endurance* the race that is set before us, looking to *Jesus . . .* " (Hebrews 12:1-2a). Notice, sin is not the only thing that can hold us back. There are weights, encumbrances that can trip up the runner. Do not allow what we have already attained to become something to distract our further progress.

Jerome (d. 420) advised his readers in regard to Philippians 3, "Put the past out of mind. Set your mind to the future. What he has reckoned perfect today he ascertains to have been false tomorrow as he reaches for better and higher goals. *By this gradual advance, never being static but always in progress,* he is able to teach us that what we supposed in our human way to be perfect still remains in some way imperfect. The only perfection is the true righteousness of God."[65]

Walk In Christ (3:17-19)

Paul now invites the Philippians to run alongside him in the race toward Christ (v. 17). As he has made steady progress in advancing his relationship to Christ, Paul now serves as an example for them to emulate. "Those" is plural, so it may be an encouragement to the Philippian leaders to not only look to Paul, but also to imitate Timothy and possibly Epaphroditus, who have already been employed as examples to copy (Phil. 2:19-30). Likewise, the Philippians can look to the mature leaders among them as examples of the race.

He then quickly pivots to those who are not imitators but enemies (v. 18). He is probably referring to the Judaizers, about whom he previously warned them, and now is repeating it to them "even with tears," emphasizing the emotional sincerity of his plea to not follow their example as "enemies of the cross of Christ" (v. 18c). What are the marks of these enemies? In verse 19 he itemizes those who are not imitators, essentially warning not to imitate them.

The end of their race is not Christ, but their own "destruction." Like the Judaizers previously mentioned, these false teachers are self-consumed, "their god is their belly," and seek self-glorification, they "glory in their shame." These individuals have only an earth-bound perspective, "minds set on earthly things." Indeed, they have swayed off course and are the *antithesis* to those who are imitating Paul's maturing toward Christ.

One critical observation needs to be made about the idea of following examples as a means of following Christ: There is a "downward spiral of imitation" with imitating Christ (2:5), to Paul (3:17a and 4:9), and then we imitate "Paul's faithful imitators"[66] (3:17b). The cautionary note is that the image of the original fades with each copy of it. As with a photocopier, copies of copies of copies are less and less clear. It is important to be followers of Christ *first*, then to learn from those who likewise follow him.

Our Citizenship (3:20-21)

Why are we not to follow the enemies' example? Because "our citizenship is in heaven" (v. 20a). Paul returns to a theme he introduced in Philippians 1:27, demonstrating citizenship through a "manner of life." Paul completes a thought regarding running the race, rejecting the false teachers, and now reminds them that their destination is not of this world! Remember, Paul was a Roman citizen and Philippi was a Roman colony. The Philippians were more Roman than Greek. Many citizens of Philippi were retired legionnaires who served for decades in the Roman military. Citizenship was at the forefront of their mind and identity. Now Paul turns this back on them.

The noun "citizenship" (*politeuma*, from where we get the word *politic*) in Philippians 3:20 is related to the verb found earlier in Philippians 1:27 "manner of life" (*politeuesthai*), each having strong political connotations, suggesting that some of the conflict within themselves and with the society was political in nature, as possibly indicated by the friction between Paul and Roman officials in Acts 16:11-40.[67] Clement of Alexandria (3rd Century A.D.) describes Christians as living "like as strangers and expatriates in the world. . . . not using the creation to satisfy our passions but high-mindedly and with thanksgiving."[68]

As citizens, Paul says we await the Savior. Of course, Paul already knew his savior, Jesus Christ, so many have understood his awaiting to be eschatological, awaiting the return of Christ in the end times. For example, when one reviews the teaching of Paul regarding the return of Christ, it can seem imminent (1 Thessalonians) or it can also seem postponed (2 Thessalonians). Either way, we live in anticipation of the return of our savior. As citizens of heaven, gathered as the church while still in the world, it makes us a colony of Christ. Philippi regarded itself as a Roman colony. Paul challenges that notion, proclaiming that as Christians we are a different identity, a colony of heaven.

Building on this eschatological theme, Paul explains that when Christ returns, he will "transform our lowly [physical] bodies" (v. 21). Paul already mentioned this earlier (see 3:11-12),and it is also found in his other epistles (cf. 1 Cor. 15:12-28). To explain, Paul does not mean just to *change*, but to be *transformed*, Greek *metaschāmatisei*. This indicates not just a change within kind, but to become a whole new creature. It's not like biological reproduction, where each reproduces "according to its kind" on the earth (Gen. 1:11), but to become something else entirely. "Therefore, if anyone is in Christ, he is a new creation. The old has passed away; behold, the new has come" (2 Cor. 5:17). Christ alone accomplishes this, not our initiative nor our efforts!

What does this say about the Judaizers? Their confidence is in themselves, their own résumé, their own efforts, which produces pride and self-centered glorification. This has no place in the Christian identity and life. There can be no compromise with them. This transformation is not because of our adherence to the teachings of Judaizers, but *only* by the power of Christ (v. 21b). *Dunamis*, translated *power*, is *not* dynamite! Yes, *dynamite* is the English word derived from Greek *dunamis*, but it is not dynamite nor some material

103

form of *destructive* power. It simply means that Christ has the ability, the strength, and energy to transform us, with nothing else or no one else required.

Therefore (4:1)

Paul concludes this section with the affirmation of relationship, calling his readers and hearers "brothers." But remember that the Greek term can also simply mean sibling, meaning brother or sister (see notes on 1:12). Echoing what he has written previously, he calls them his "joy and crown," offering praise of the quality of their relationship and sense of achievement this congregation represents to Paul. Given the relative success or failure in other congregations, e.g. Thessalonica and Corinth, Philippi's congregation represents a spiritual success, a crowning achievement for Paul's mission in Macedonia.

What is his closing message to them? "Stand firm thus in the Lord" (4:1). Sound familiar? This has been a subtext throughout the letter, articulated with different words and imagery, but consistently present.

INSIGHTS FROM THE TEXT

Paul encourages the Philippians to stand firm in their faith, keep advancing on the goal, and not be swayed by those who would oppose them. He once again reminds the overseers and deacons of their unique posture toward leadership, one that will set them apart and keep them on the right track, never looking back, always pressing forward.

Leaders Are Paradoxical. David Gray writes that, in comparison to the worldly connotations of leadership, emphasizing personal power, position, and title, Philippians 2:5-11 is "a paradox relative to the traditional beliefs of leadership,"[69] i.e. servanthood. The Apostle Paul continues to present a paradoxical picture of leadership in Philippians 3:13-14, where leadership is portrayed as an upward call with downward mobility.[70] Philippi is not Corinth! Paul's opponents describe themselves as super-apostles (2 Cor. 11:5), seeking personal gain, prominence, and higher position. Yet, even in Corinth, Paul expresses the paradoxical leadership he sees, "Indeed, I consider that I am not in the least inferior to these super-apostles." Paul essentially boasts about his inferiority, something unheard of in contemporary leadership, but he was no less a leader because of it.

Leaders Focus on Eternity. Paul appeals to his eschatology to underscore his approach to Christian life and leadership. I know it is popular to use phrases like, "I'm *pan*-millennial. It's all going to *pan out* in the end" or "I'm *pro*millennial . . . I don't know what's going to happen, but I'm *all for it!*" This may be quaint, and even defuse some tense theological moments, but it is equally inadequate. It is not the purpose of this book to engage in eschatological dialog or advocate a particular view of the end times.[71] However, without a definitive statement regarding eschatology, the end times, the story of Scripture seems to conclude nebulously, without substantial detail. Knowing how our story ends is not optional; it's critical.

Paul appeals to Christ's return as a source of distinction as one who is a citizen of Christ, one who is advancing in the race, and avoiding the example of the false teachers. We can stand firm because we not only see the immediate goal, but also our eternal goal with Christ. When we lead with eternity on our mind, it places earthly matters in perspective, and prioritizes matters of the Spirit. Knowing what is yet to come also gives leaders hope in times of desperation, persecution, or as in Paul's circumstance, opposition.

Leaders Make Spiritual Progress. I can appreciate Paul's candor. He explains that he is perpetually moving forward toward maturity in Christ, but knows he has not yet attained it, nor will he fully attain it until eternity. Yet, he continues to strive, to have progress in his spiritual life.

Geometry has a theorem that is insightful here: *asymptote*. It is a geometry term, but when used generally it simply means always advancing, always pursuing, but never actually achieving (Figure 7.1). Consider this, if someone is standing 10 feet from a wall, but I tell them they can only take steps half the distance from the wall, while they will approach the wall, getting closer and closer with each step, they will never reach the wall. They would go from 10' to 5', then from 5' to 2.5', then to 1.25', then to about 7", but the number would never reach 0, because they are only moving half the distance to the wall, never the full distance. Of course, being so close to the wall is in fact close enough.

This geometric theorem echoes the principles in Philippians 3:14, not yet having achieved, but always making progress. No one is 100% mature! The notion that a leader has to be literally perfect, well, there is no such requirement and no such person. It reminds us we all have room for improvement! But this is no excuse for stagnation, settling, or swaying.

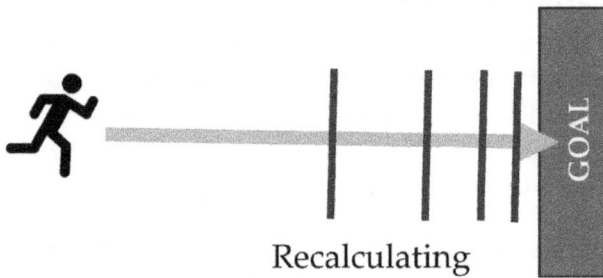

Recalculating

Figure 7.1

Leaders Lead by Influence. Leadership is often mistaken for a position or title, like making elder-overseer or deacon nothing more than a place holder on an organizational chart. That is *not* leadership. At best that is management. The simple fact is that leadership means one has influence, the capability of changing circumstances by affecting and prompting people to join them in their mission. Leaders exert influence any time they are in the community. Even leadership development is a matter of directed influence. If they are connected to people, they exert influence. The question is what kind of influence they exert. Do they exert negative influence, creating movement away from progress and growth, and lose what has already been attained? Or, do they exert positive influence, creating motivation and encouragement for perpetual advancement toward Christ?

Paul appeals to the Philippians to race along with him in his spiritual life and ministry, to follow the example of Christ, himself, and other leaders around them. When we do this intentionally, it becomes part of discipleship of our peers as well as the next generation of Christian leaders.

Leaders Are Christians First. Dr. David Roadcup of TCMI is a friend and colleague. We have known one another, in a variety of capacities, for over 40 years. He is indeed a disciple-maker, but he is also a leadership coach. In an article, Roadcup wrote, "In his book *Disciple,* Juan Carlos Ortiz says the greatest problem facing the church today is 'the perpetual childhood of the believer.' The fact that most of our churches are made up of spiritually immature believers is a major issue to the church fulfilling her mission. This extreme lack of spiritual development continually cripples the dynamic advancement of our churches.'"[72] How many times is *being* a believer an *assumption* rather than a starting point? Being a Christian, even a member of the church, has to be more than just checking the qualifications box. When we consider someone for leadership, elder or deacon, and they are vetted for the role, do we ask about their conversion, how they came to Christ, their personal testimony? Perhaps ask what they do to continue forming their relationship with Jesus. The Apostle Paul assumes that leaders are *influencers* and should be *imitated*, meaning they must grow up in Christ!

PERSONAL & TEAM REFLECTION

1. What encourages you to stand firm, continue the race, and make forward progress regardless of the circumstances?

2. What influences distract you, sway you from the course?

3. How could you be a more positive influence as a leader on those around you? What is one change (add or subtract) you could make to improve your influence?

4. Regarding your spiritual progress as a leader, beyond attending worship, have you done the following? (☑ each that applies)

   ☐ Read a Christian book

   ☐ Attended a Christian conference

   ☐ Subscribed to a Christian journal

   ☐ Participated in an accountability group

   ☐ Practiced spiritual disciplines

   ☐ Other: _____

5. Who could you ask to "run" alongside you in the race? Whom could you mentor into leadership?

Chapter 8

Peace vs. Hostilities (4:2-9)

"Duck and cover!" I remember doing practice drills in school in the event of a nuclear exchange with our mortal enemy, the Soviet Union. It was the Cold War, when both sides of the world were poised on the brink of destruction. Our official policy was called M.A.D., **M**utually **A**ssured **D**estruction, proposing that stockpiling more nuclear weapons would deter our enemies from launching an attack. In high school, I was enrolled in a required course called "Civil Defense," to raise awareness of the threats and how to survive nuclear annihilation (a bit of an oxymoron), such as determining how fast it would take to reach the closest fallout shelter. FYI: We would not have made it. For decades we literally prepared for global thermonuclear war.

However, by the 1970s we gave up on the idea of *peace* with the Soviet Union and settled for a lesser achievement, *détente*, which in French means *relaxation*. Unlike peace, which presumes a mutually positive and beneficial relationship between parties; *détente* simply required a lack of hostility. We don't have to love each other; we don't even have to like each other; we just leave each other alone. It definitely lowered the bar of expectations for international diplomacy.

Have you ever been in a congregation that has settled for *détente*? No open hostilities, not conflict that one would immediately notice. But, no sense or experience of love in the ethos of the church. The occasional odd glance from across the lobby, the silence as people pass in a hallway, hushed comments made to others, and of course making sure we don't sit near "them" in worship. *Détente!* We don't have to love each other; we don't even have to like each other; we just leave one another alone.

In this section, Paul brings up a desire for *peace* by resolving interpersonal conflict (vv. 2-3), relating to God (vv. 4-7), and ensuring internal personal harmony (vv. 8-9). Paul describes the process of attaining God's peace, in all its dimensions, as an intentional choice of believers and their leaders. As leaders in Christ' body, do we actively seek to enable peace and resolve conflict, or do we settle for *détente* and fuel conflict?

THE TEXT

Philippians 4:2-9 4 I entreat Euodia and I entreat Syntyche to agree in the Lord. 3 Yes, I ask you also, true companion [*sudzuge*], help these women, who have labored side by side with me in the gospel together with Clement and the rest of my fellow workers, whose names are in the book of life. 4 Rejoice in the Lord always; again I will say, Rejoice. 5 Let your reasonableness [*epieikes*] be known to everyone. The Lord is at hand; 6 do not be anxious about anything, but in everything by prayer and supplication with thanksgiving let your requests be made known to God. 7 And the peace of God, which surpasses all understanding, will guard [*phrourāsei*] your hearts and your minds in Christ Jesus.

8 Finally, brothers, whatever is true, whatever is honorable, whatever is just, whatever is pure, whatever is lovely, whatever is commendable, if there is any excellence, if there is anything worthy of praise, think [*logizomai*] about these things. 9 What you have learned and received [*paralabete*] and heard and seen in me—practice these things, and the God of peace will be with you.

TEXT QUESTIONS

- What does Paul urge Euodia and Syntyche to do in Philippians 4:2, and how does he address the issues?
- How can we apply Paul's plea for unity between Euodia and Syntyche (v. 2) to our conflicts and disagreements?
- In Philippians 4:3, whom does Paul ask to help Euodia and Syntyche, and what is the reason for his request?

- In what ways does Paul's encouragement to rejoice in the Lord *always* (v. 4) challenge our understanding of joy, especially in difficult circumstances?
- What types of things does Paul encourage the Philippians to focus on in Philippians 4:8, and what is the expected outcome?
- What does it mean to think about whatever is true, honorable, just, pure, lovely, and commendable?

INTO THE TEXT

The opening verses of chapter 4 reflect earlier sentiments of the letter (1:27, 2:2). Paul is reaching the conclusion of his letter to the Philippians. Before engaging the text itself, just a note on the value of conclusions in Paul's letters. While some people give little attention to the final portion of his letters, scholars pour over them with a virtual microscope. Often the conclusion has a wealth of personal information absent from the body of the letter. Paul also often includes valuable geographical references (4:15-16) and refers to other individuals (4:2, 3, 18) that aid in reconstructing the sequence of events in the first century. Finally, most of Paul's letters conclude as a practical summary, providing balance to his theologically laden message.

In the previous chapter, 4:1 was treated as a transitional statement, it both concludes the previous section and opens this one. His admonition to "stand firm" and repeating that they are his "joy and crown" take on new meaning. The immediate context, standing firm, becomes the basis for advancing the peace of the church despite interpersonal conflict and individual struggles.

Resolving Conflict (4:2-3)

Euodia and Syntyche are immortalized in the biblical text as two individuals embroiled in conflict serious enough to warrant Paul's attention. In 4:2, Paul gives the instruction to "think the same way," which is also the injunction he gave in 2:2. It is a refrain that has both positive (2:5, 3:15) and negative (3:15, 19) implications for disagreement in the church.[73] Notice, Paul does not *command*, but entreats, requests, each of them, not just one of them, to settle their dispute. Conflict is rarely unidirectional and typically *both* parties need to address it, such as seems to be the case here.

Euodia and Syntyche are not being called out as the bad ones, *berated* by name; such as Diotrephes (3 Jn. 9) or Demas (2 Tim. 4:10). Rather, Paul identifies them as long-term coworkers, friends, leaders, readily recognized by the Philippian church. Euodia and Syntyche are described as having "labored side by side with me [Paul]," similar to those described in 1:27. Along with them, Paul mentions "Clement" by name and "fellow workers," who are not listed in his letter, but whose names are written in the "book of life." What he asks them to do is what he needs the entire congregation to do: become one-minded.

While Paul does not indicate the source of their conflict, nor does he elaborate on the level of conflict they have reached, the situation does require third party intervention (v. 3). He describes this individual as a "true companion" [*sudzuge*]. Some have suggested that this could in fact be a proper name, Synzgous, as footnoted in most modern translations. Speculation abounded in the ancient church as to the identify of this individual, so much so that several early church authorities had to debunk the rumors of their day, such as Theodoret saying that 4:3 refers to Paul's wife, or possibly as Marcus Victorinus suggested that it was Epaphroditus, who is described similarly but not identically.[74]

Prior to departing this section of the text, I raise two main cautions regarding Euodia and Syntyche. Frank Thielman of Beeson Divinity School warns that: (1) Some have tried to rewrite the biblical text to make Euodia a male, Euodias, and hence the husband of Syntyche, and their dispute a marital one. Hence, it hopes to completely avoid the appearance of women in the ministry or leadership of the church. In fact, the King James Version translates it as such, essentially covering the matter from view to those who don't know Greek! (2) Others err the opposite direction and *overstate* the contents of the text, building from inference alone that these women were in fact elders or other church leaders.[75] The truth probably exists in the center of this spectrum. Nonetheless, Paul seeks the resolution of their conflict for their own good, the good of the leadership team, and the peace of the congregation.

Relating to God (4:4-7)

Once again, Paul affirms the Philippians as the cause for his joy, twice exhorting them to rejoice with him! But, not due to their own accomplishments or their successes, but to "rejoice in the Lord always" (v. 4). He has encouraged Euodia and Syntyche to find peace "in the Lord" (v. 2) and now the congregation is to rejoice "in the Lord" (v. 4). If you want to stand firm in the bond of peace, it has to be "in the Lord," not yourselves!

Paul then offers several propositions coalescing into "the peace of God" (v. 7). First, he affirms their "reasonableness" [epieikes], elsewhere translated "gentleness," as a quality of their community (v. 5). This same word is used in 1 Timothy 3:3 to describe the qualities of an overseer, as well as in James 3:17 of "peaceable" based on "wisdom from above." Basically, the word conveys a quality of community building, a quality worth being "known to everybody" (4:5). This level of community building is not achieved by human effort, an individual or a congregation, but because of the presence of Jesus Christ, "the Lord is at hand." Paul says, "the Lord is at hand," appealing again to the imminent eschatological presence of the person of Jesus Christ. Holding to that expectation will achieve peace, not individual or congregational efforts.

Paul then offers an admonition to address their anxiety (4:6). I once saw a sign out front of a general store that read, "Humans are 90% water – basically, cucumbers with anxiety." It may appear that he is just instructing *not* to "be anxious about anything," but he follows up this instruction with a means of achieving it. Paul's instruction leans on a simple yet profound premise. Anxiety occurs when we rely on ourselves; peace reigns when we rely on God. The Philippians are told to choose peace over anxiety, to rely on God rather than self. This is accomplished "by prayer and supplication with thanksgiving;" we can place all our concerns in the presence of the One who gives peace, especially concerns that are obviously beyond our control. Anxiety only occurs when we are in a situation, circumstance, or assigned a task or goal for which we feel inadequate, overwhelmed. God, in whom Paul instructs us to place our requests, is not inadequate for any of these. To be clear, Paul is not saying "do nothing, anxiety will dissipate on its own," nor is he suggesting "my best and God does the rest," rather he is offering a constructive action for every occasion of anxiety. What is the result? Paul promises that they will have the "peace of God" (4:7). He identifies this peace with several descriptors. First, like prayer, it is centered on God and for this reason it is beyond human understanding. Since it is *not* built on self-reliance, it cannot be comprehended in human terms, but only discerned spiritually. This peace will serve to "guard" [*phrourāsei*] (4:7b). The term does not refer to the activity of a soldier, but is still a military term, like a *gate keeper*, controlling what comes in and goes out. That is what the peace of God does, it *regulates*, it does not leave our anxieties unchecked.

God's peace guards rather comprehensively, "your hearts and minds in Christ Jesus" (4:7b). In the ancient world a variety of opinion existed over the role and function of the heart and brain, as well as what they represented. However, in the Greco-Roman period, the time in which Paul was writing, the heart was understood as the seat of emotion and source of life, and the brain (mind) was its regulator, working in conjunction with one another. However, "For thousands of years, it was believed that only through the heart could one connect with God."[76] Perhaps this is why Paul mentions the heart and then the mind (brain).

Figure 8.1 illustrates the instructions Paul provided toward securing the peace of God in our lives. The progression seems obvious, from settling interpersonal conflicts, with the assistance of other faithful coworkers, spend time rejoicing in the Lord, lay aside our anxieties in favor of prayer, so that we can enter the peace of God.

One major observation: Entering God's peace is *not* automatic. Failure at any of these levels can disrupt it, but we can experience it when we follow Paul's prescription with care.

Peace of God that Guards Our
Heart, Minds, and Actions (4:7, 9)

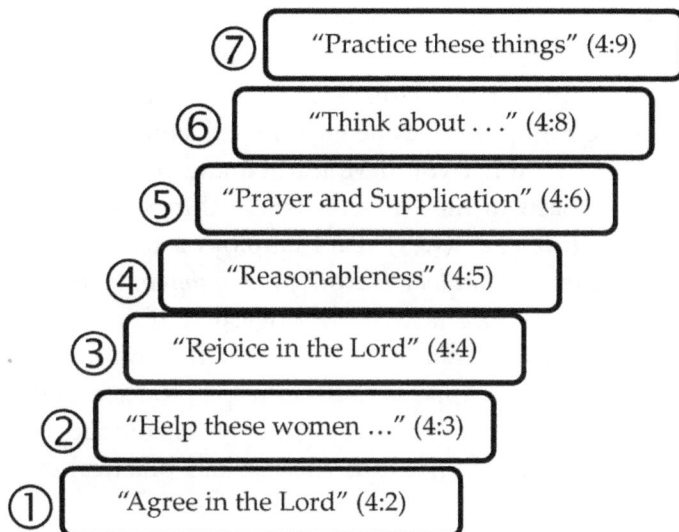

⑦ | "Practice these things" (4:9)

⑥ | "Think about . . ." (4:8)

⑤ | "Prayer and Supplication" (4:6)

④ | "Reasonableness" (4:5)

③ | "Rejoice in the Lord" (4:4)

② | "Help these women ..." (4:3)

① | "Agree in the Lord" (4:2)

Figure 8.1

Personal Harmony (4:8-9)

Paul concludes this particular section on the peace of God with the premise that virtues drive out the vices, as one increases, the other decreases. Once again, he uses the word "Finally" (v. 8), and then describes a mindset, "Think [*logizomai*] about these things" (v. 8i) and the subsequent behaviors; habits that will form, "practice these things" (v. 9b), given the promised result that "the God of peace will be with you" (v. 9c). In v. 8 *logizomai* is translated *think*, but elsewhere it is reckon, consider, or reason. Our usual take on the verse, "think nice thoughts," does not do justice to Paul's use of *logizomai*. "Reckon or evaluate these things" feels more substantial in the text and leads more easily to what he says next in vs. 9, that is, evaluating and making decisions based on these things facilitates practicing what they have learned from Paul, then they will have God's peace.

Essentially, Paul moves from heart and mind to head and hand. As a Christian educator, these outcomes reflect holistic learning: cognitive (mind), affective (heart), and active (hands). What is this mindset? With the prefix of "whatever is," he lists the focus of the mature Christian mind: true, honorable, just, pure, lovely, commendable, excellent, and anything worthy of praise. Note that *honorable* is used of deacons in 1 Timothy 3:8, and of old and young Christian men on Crete (Titus 2:2, 7), translated *dignified*. Paul encourages the Philippians, as he encouraged Timothy in the letters sent to him, that "What you have learned and received [*paralabete*] and heard and seen in me—practice these things, and the God of peace will be with you" (v. 9). Paul employs a term often used in educational contexts, *paralabete,* from *paralambanō.* It implies a fixed content; in this instance a fixed theological tradition is what they have learned from Paul and his colaborers.[77] Beyond his instruction to them, he once again appeals to his example, learned-and-received and heard-and-seen in me. Once again, he encourages imitation, combining the value of verbal instruction and practical example of Christian practices.

INSIGHTS FROM THE TEXT

Leaders Engage Conflict Directly. In reference to Euodia and Syntyche, Jeramie Rinne wrote, "Elders don't turn a blind eye to strife between members in hopes that it will fix itself. It rarely does. You may be tempted to avoid and ignore, because you're a normal person who doesn't enjoy breaking up fights. . . . Conflicts present incredible opportunities for people to grow in Christ."[78] It starts with you! It is unfortunate that after 2000 years, all we know of Euodia and Syntyche is that they seem to be troublemakers rather than peacemakers like Clement. From what little we know about the catalytic situation that produced the conflict between Euodia and Syntyche, Clement had nothing to do with the conflict. Paul "entreats" them to settle their dispute, but *not* Clement. However, Clement is asked to step into a situation that apparently didn't directly involve him and become the peacemaker Paul needed him to be.

Emotionally and spiritually, no one likes conflict. If someone did, I'd be a little concerned. We all have a natural tendency to avoid tense and awkward situations when there is obviously a quarrel between individuals. However, peacemakers sense a matter of higher importance, something more important than quarrel and dispute, more important than their ease and comfort, and they step into the situation not for their own benefit, but the higher purpose. In this case, the text emphasizes that the work of advancing the gospel and peace within the community of faith has been distracted due to this conflict, so Paul says to settle the matter "in the Lord" and describes them as co-laborers that now need to focus on their mission.

Leaders Avoid Distractions. Paul's two main concerns seem to be steadfastness to the gospel and the unity of the church. His priorities were to build congregations that reflected their mission and identity, that is, being and doing *church*. Conflict distracts from this and tends lead us to hyperfocus on what is often a minor matter magnified beyond reason. Remember Paul's call for "reasonableness" (v. 5)? One significant lesson that leaders can learn from Euodia and Syntyche is to avoid petty differences that can divert you from your mission and ministry.

When we learn to prioritize matters, exercising discernment, knowing what is essential and what is opinion, recognizing what is worth having a conflict over and what is of no significance, we can live with the differences. When we fail to do this, anything will become a distraction and potential source of conflict. A veteran pastor once gave me a piece of folk wisdom, "If we were busy doing all the things we *should* be doing we wouldn't have the time to do the things we *shouldn't* be doing." Sometimes it's not a matter of right or wrong, good or bad, but just important and unimportant.

Leaders Manage Their Mindset. Paul desired leaders, and all believers, to experience the peace of God. This is not a philosophical worldview, psychological condition, or an intellectual achievement, but the fruit that is borne from a mature relationship with Jesus Christ. We experience God's peace when we choose to live our lives, centering our heart, mind, and hands on Him. The opposite of His peace is *anxiety*, a mental state that is anything but peaceful, a fixation on ourselves or a circumstance. How do we minimize anxiety and move into God's peace? Figure 8.2 illustrates three instructions given by Paul in this section of Philippians 4.

First, *horizontally*, address interpersonal conflict (4:2-3). It is difficult to have the peace of God when not in harmony with one another. Second, *vertically*, grow in your relationship with God, through prayer and supplication to Him (4:4-7). Once again, communicating with the One who is offering peace removes anxiety. Finally, *internally*, fill your mind with godly thoughts, resulting in godly actions (4:8-9). We cannot choose the circumstances of our lives and ministries. Our church may be less than ideal and even plagued with issues. But we do have a choice of mindset. Do we focus on the conflict or on Christ? Do we become worrisome about circumstances beyond our control or turn it over to the Lord? Do we fill our minds with troubling thoughts or with godly matters, with obvious results? We can choose to be peacemakers who experience the peace of God!

Figure 8.2

Women Can Be Leaders. Yes, this is somewhat of a controversial idea. That is true, regardless of how it is received in many churches today. Besides Paul's description of Euodia and Syntyche, it is evident that women were engaged in doing ministry within the church (Prisca, Acts 18:2-3/Rom. 16:3; Phoebe, Rom. 16:1-2; Lydia, Acts 16:14-15; Junia, Rom. 16:7). The question is to what degree were they involved? Did they have an "official" function in the church? What kind of leadership did they exercise? As Wendy Cotter observed, "The respect Paul exhibits toward each woman's position, and the level of concern he shows in making a public appeal to them suggests that both Euodia and Syntyche hold some office of distinction in the Philippian Community."[79] Perhaps they were deacons, or perhaps they were just very respected, engaged members of the congregation who now find themselves in disagreement.

Regardless, they are yet one more example of women partners in ministry with Paul.

There is little debate regarding the presence of women deacons in the church. They have been present in the church since the first century. It was only in the early 20th century that their legitimacy was questioned, coinciding with the advent of the women's suffrage movement, women's right to vote, the rise of the corporate board structure in congregational governance, and the arrival of classical liberalism.[80] Purely in the realm of speculation, if they were deacons, perhaps Clement was either a co-deacon or even an elder, whom Paul instructs to become a third-party peacemaker between them.

PERSONAL & TEAM REFLECTION

1. What are the results of unchecked conflict in the church? Among the leadership team? Has your congregation ever experienced this? What happened?

2. What would it take for you to become a better peacemaker, one who actively resolves conflict?

3. What makes you anxious in your life or congregation? Identify this item. Now, perhaps pray for it daily for 30 days. Write your prayers in a journal and invite others to join you.

4. Reflect on Figures 8.1 and 8.2 and the commentary about them. Given these measures to secure the peace of God, which one is your "weakest" component? Where is there room for improvement? Identify two ways you can address this.

5. In regard to women in your congregation, what roles and functions do they play in the church's ministry? Rather than asking, "What *can't* they do?" explore "What *can* they do?"

Chapter 9

Supporting Stewards vs. Selfish Managers (4:10-23)

Legendary British preacher Charles H. Spurgeon (1834-1892), known as the "Prince of Preachers," was an incredible wordsmith. He was also recognized for his thought-provoking sermon illustrations. One illustration that is frequently attributed to him is "The Carrot and the Horse." It unfolds a story about a gardener who presented his king with the greatest, largest, and most perfect carrot he had ever grown in his garden. The king is touched by his generosity and grants the gardener a large parcel of land in reward. A nearby nobleman who witnesses this event, especially the King's kind gesture toward the gardener, decided it would be personally advantageous *for him* to likewise present the king a gift, the finest horse from his stable. Upon receiving the horse, the king simply expressed his gratitude for the horse and nothing more. The nobleman was confused and in frustration asked the king to explain himself, why a mere thanks and no gift? The king replied, "That gardener was giving *me* the carrot. But you were giving *yourself* the horse."[81] Generosity isn't about you, it's about the one to whom you give the gift.

Paul praises the Philippians' generosity in their financial support of his ministry. Certainly, the leadership of the congregation, overseers and deacons, had a significant part in getting Paul his much-needed funds. Presumably, however, even this was met with opposition from within the congregation as well as from other congregations who did not support him. Some practiced generosity while others bordered on greed. Leaders are either going to be supportive stewards of what God has entrusted to them or become selfish managers, hoarding their financial resources for no pastoral purpose.

THE TEXT

Philippians 4:10-23 10 I rejoiced in the Lord greatly that now at length you have revived your concern for me. You were indeed concerned for me, but you had no opportunity [*ākaireisthe*]. 11 Not that I am speaking of being in need, for I have learned in whatever situation I am to be content. 12 I know how to be brought low, and I know how to abound. In any and every circumstance, I have learned the secret of facing plenty and hunger, abundance and need. 13 I can do all things through him who strengthens me.

14 Yet it was kind of you to share my trouble. 15 And you Philippians yourselves know that in the beginning of the gospel, when I left Macedonia, no church entered into partnership with me in giving and receiving, except you only. 16 Even in Thessalonica you sent me help for my needs once and again. 17 Not that I seek the gift, but I seek the fruit that increases to your credit. 18 I have received full payment, and more. I am well supplied, having received from Epaphroditus the gifts you sent, a fragrant offering, a sacrifice acceptable and pleasing to God. 19 And my God will supply every need of yours according to his riches in glory in Christ Jesus. 20 To our God and Father be glory forever and ever. Amen.

21 Greet every saint in Christ Jesus. The brothers who are with me greet you. 22 All the saints greet you, especially those of Caesar's household.

23 The grace of the Lord Jesus Christ be with your spirit.

TEXT QUESTIONS

- In Philippians 4:10, what does Paul express joy over, and what change does he notice in the Philippians' attitude toward him?
- What does Paul say in Philippians 4:11-12 about his attitude toward his circumstances, and what has he learned through his experience?

- In what ways does Paul's declaration that he can do all things through the one who strengthens him (v. 13) encourage us to rely on our faith in times of struggle or doubt?
- In Philippians 4:15-16, how does Paul describe the support he received from the Philippians during his ministry?
- What significance do you find in Paul's closing remarks about the grace of the Lord Jesus Christ (v. 23), and how can we embody this grace in our interactions with others as we conclude our gatherings or discussions?
- How does Paul conclude his letter in Philippians 4:19-20, and what does he say God will provide for the Philippians?

INTO THE TEXT

Paul expresses his sincere appreciation for the Philippians' continued financial support for his ministry, especially while he is incarcerated in Rome. But, from where could opposition arise? Why would anyone oppose it? *Fear, a lack of Christ-centered contentment.* Those who want to keep their resources for themselves so they can use it their own way, to maintain what they presently have, fearful of the circumstances of their life changing and being in need, not believing the Lord would provide. Yes, this portion of the text is directly regarding the finances of the church. Paul will employ the vocabulary and metaphors of commerce in this section. Without a doubt the leadership of the Philippian church will need to hear this, as they are ultimately responsible for financial decisions and disbursement.

The conclusion of Paul's letter seems to parallel the letter's opening, using the same or similar words as well as the almost parallel order of comments made, as Thompson and Longenecker note.[82]

Conclusion	Introduction
"I rejoice in the Lord" (4:10)	"with joy" (1:4)
To think about me (4:10)	"to think about you" (1:7)
Partners in affliction (4:14)	Partners in grace (1:7)
You partnered (4:15)	Partnership (1:5)

With this Paul comes full circle, affirming his joy, his relationship with the Philippians, and their partnership and participation in his ministry.

Thermometer or Thermostat? (4:10-13)

Paul's joy is not based on the Philippians' gifts, the provision for his needs, but in their partnership (v. 10) and in the Lord (vv. 11-13). This is contrary to what the Stoic philosophers taught, advocating contentment through *self*-sufficiency. Here, Paul argues for the sufficiency of Christ and reliance on Him to meet his needs.[83]

Philippians 4:10-11 reflects on the Philippians support given to Paul, *but* were impeded from sending a gift, but have *now* resumed their support for Paul. He uses the term *ākaireisthe*, "having no opportunity," which is in the middle voice, meaning it was not they who impeded the opportunity; they were somehow blocked from having an adequate opportunity. They encountered some form of opposition, internal or external, some obstacle to their generosity, but that has now been removed. The early church father Chrysostom (d. A.D. 407) said of them in v. 10, "He [Paul] sees that it is impossible to give precise instructions about everything – their going out, their coming in, their words, their inner condition and their company. All of these a Christian must think about in context. He [Paul] says concisely and as it were in a nutshell" to follow his example.[84]

Paul's contentment "in any and every circumstance" (v. 11) and his affirmation that he "can do all things through him who strengthens me" (v. 13) once again underscores his ultimate dependence and reliance on Jesus Christ to sustain him in all circumstances and demands of his ministry. Paul's life is one of stable contentment in spite of turbulent circumstances. The principle is simple to illustrate. Thermometers *react* to the temperature in their context, rising and lowering depending on the ambient heat or lack of heat in the room. A thermometer doesn't control the temperature, it just reports it. However, a thermostat is more advanced! It not only can detect the temperature, but can then influence it, it can cool or heat the area to a prescribed temperature. It maintains a preset temperature *regardless* of the context, it is stable. Leaders, mature Christians, need to be thermostats, not thermometers! We need to be content in all circumstances through our relationship with Jesus Christ, and draw from that the ability to fulfill our ministries in all circumstances.

When we are content, we are motivated to be generous. When we are not content, we have reason to fear and to hoard our resources. Philippi was a church that was generous; like Paul they rejoiced in his ministry and mission, the advance of the gospel, partnering with him, even in this difficult period of his life.

The Philippians' Legacy (4:14-20)

While the Philippians sent a monetary gift, Paul continues to offer affirmation for their ministry. For him their real gift was not monetary, rather it was their partnership in the gospel (vv. 14-17). He explains that they have shared in his troubles, the advancement of the gospel, and his ministry. On a personal, and insightful, note, Paul compares the faithful support of the Philippians for this missionary work in Macedonia,[85] noting that they were his solitary supporter for that endeavor (v. 15). He then said the same of his mission to Thessalonica (v. 16);[86] the Philippians continued to provide support for his ministry. It should be noted that the churches of Macedonia and Thessalonica would become supporters of Paul's later mission work, mirroring the faithful support of the Philippians. *Generosity begets generosity.* It is in vv. 14-20 that Paul employs a business metaphor, using the language of commerce to describe their relationship, such as credit (v. 17) and full payment (v. 18).

However, Paul also employs the language of sacrifice to describe their gift. He was not requesting additional support (v. 17). He describes their gift as being all he expected, their "full payment." He expected no more from them, as he said earlier, he was lacking in nothing because of their support. He continues to describe the gift delivered by Epaphroditus as a "fragrant offering," a phrase frequently used to describe sacrifices (Gen. 8:21; Lev. 1:9, 13, 17). Without suggesting *quid pro quo*, Paul offers the Philippians a doxology, expressing that just as their gift has fulfilled Paul's needs, so now God "will supply every need of yours" (vv. 19-20). Just as Paul opened with rejoicing in the Lord (v. 10), he now glorifies God, offering the

"Amen," which is both an affirmation, meaning "truly" or "verily," but also a statement of desire, "let it be so."

Farewell to Philippi (4:21-23)

We come to Paul's final words to the Philippians. He doesn't write a second letter to them, although he probably did visit them as occasion gave opportunity; but these are his last recorded words to them. He urges them to "Greet every *saint*" (v. 21a), using the same word as in Philippians 1:1. Though he is under home incarceration Paul is not alone in sending this letter, as he mentions "the brothers" in v. 21b. He sends the Philippians greetings from all the saints that his ministry has touched in Rome, many made possible by the support from the Philippians, but "especially those of Caesar's household" (vv. 21b, 22), which was addressed also in Philippians 1:15, 17. Caesar's household does not mean the "imperial family," i.e. Caesar himself and his family, but the household included all of those who were in the home, including servants and slaves (see Eph. 5:21-6:9). His final words are, "The grace of the Lord Jesus Christ be with your spirit."

INSIGHTS FROM THE TEXT

Leaders Are Generous. While leaders are charged to be faithful stewards of the church's resources, this does not mean to adopt a practice of needlessly hording resources that could be put to better use. Like the Philippians, congregations that are directed by faithful leaders practice generosity within the congregation, to the Kingdom work beyond their walls, and to the community in which they minister. "And let us not grow weary of doing good, for in due season we will reap, if we do not give up. So then, as we have opportunity, let us do good to everyone, and especially to those who are of the household of faith" (Gal. 6:9-10). Generosity is grounded on the acknowledgment of God's provision to us, and in turn our desire to share that provision with others. When we fail to be generous, defaulting to a practical greed, it is often rooted in the false notion that it is *not* God who has provided, rather *I* have provided for *myself*. Servant leaders are indeed generous.

Leaders Have Positive Contentment. For those of us who are married and can remember the wedding vows, the traditional verbiage asks both groom and bride to promise faithfulness to one another, "for better or for worse, in sickness and in health, for richer or poorer." It is an affirmation that their relationship and commitment to one another is not circumstantial or temporary, but a covenant between them and God.

Paul speaks of his *unconditional contentment* in Christ! Regardless of the circumstances, even in his incarceration, he would continue to fulfill the ministry that Jesus had appointed to him. He would not just settle for contentment, which can still have a poor attitude, *but* Paul expresses contentment with a positive attitude, even exhibiting gratitude for what God has provided. Do not misunderstand, this is not a call to reckless abandon of financial stewardship or for not challenging people to grow in their financial support in ministry, settling for status quo. Rather, it reminds us that whatever the Lord has provided, *He has provided for a reason*, and we should *never* cease or suspend our ministry due to a *perceived* absence of provision. Yes, it may require a congregation's leaders to reassess what can be accomplished or the pace at which they can do ministry, but it does not serve as permission to pause.

Leaders Support Ministry Financially. We place a premium on ministry, not money! It is relatively easy to find a church "leader" speak eloquently about the need for ministry and the opportunities readily available for the ministry of their congregation, even offer prayer support, but who fail to support it financially. No, leaders are active financial supporters of ministry. Yes, prayer, volunteering, and sacrificing time are greatly appreciated, but leaders need to support the church's mission and ministry with their finances. Congregations need to follow leaders who are actively giving financially to the church.

Leaders, as the supervisors of the congregation's financial resources, reflect their primary commitments in the budget, a predetermined set up priorities as reflected in the budget. A contemporary proverb says, "If I want to know your priorities, let me see your checkbook." Of course, most don't use checkbooks anymore, but how about an audit of how your spending reflects your priorities?

Leaders See Gospel Potential. God provided Paul with financial support to take his second missionary journey, which resourced him to reach Philippi and plant that congregation. Now the Philippians have supplied Paul's needs to travel even further, planting congregations in Macedonia and Thessalonica. An old axiom that remains relevant today is that *people don't give to budgets, they give to do ministry.* The Philippians gave generously, supported Paul's mission not just because they were his friends, but because they wanted to be his partners in advancing the gospel. They saw the potential his mission had for advancing the message of Jesus Christ throughout the world, and now even in the Imperial capital, Rome, and wanted to partner with him. When we give, we magnify and multiply our ministry, and become part of that mission.

Leaders Lead Leaders. Yes, it is the thread that runs throughout the entire letter.[87] The overseers and deacons of the Philippian church are leaders who were trained by other leaders, who had been trained by leaders, all who exemplify Christ as their ultimate example of leadership. Paul's continual admonition to live as servant leaders and learn by imitation is once again echoed in the conclusion of his letter. If you want to learn how to be a leader, find a leader to mentor you, learn from them, and follow Christ as they follow him. The same is applicable to the leadership team. Commit to the development of the individuals in the team and the team as the congregation's leadership. Ministries such as e2:effective elders (e2elders.org) are committed to aiding leadership teams to develop to their full potential, equipping leaders to lead well.

PERSONAL & TEAM REFLECTION

1. How do you foster generosity in the congregation? How is it exemplified as a value for others to exhibit?

2. If your personal budget, or your "checkbook," were reviewed, what would it say about your priorities?

3. Similarly, if your church's budget, or its "checkbook," were reviewed, what would it say about your priorities?

4. What is a ministry initiative you have considered doing but has been delayed? Why? What would it take to launch it?

5. If your team could emulate another team, who might it be? How?

Epilogue

Did Paul visit the Philippians again? Paul does not die at the end of Acts 28. Early church tradition dating back to c. A.D. 95 suggests that upon his release from a first Roman imprisonment he engaged in yet another mission trip, one that occurred post-Acts. Philippi was indeed one of his destinations for that trip! Paul wrote the Philippians of his intention to return to them in Philippians 2:23-24, "I hope therefore to send him [Timothy] just as soon as I see how it will go with me, 24 and I trust in the Lord that shortly *I myself will come also.*" This final visit to Philippi may be implied by Paul's statement to Timothy in 1 Timothy 1:3, "As I urged you when I was going to *Macedonia*, remain at Ephesus so that you may charge certain persons not to teach any different doctrine. . . ." In fact, the *NIV Study Bible* has a map of Paul's "Fourth Missionary Journey" in its treatment of the Pastoral Epistles (1-2 Timothy and Titus) with Philippi identified as a destination.[88]

Did Paul make such a journey, a fourth missionary trip? It is speculative, but consistent with Paul's desire to return to them and suggested in the earliest of church traditions. Also, it seems fitting that Paul would visit "all the saints in Christ Jesus who are at Philippi, with the overseers and deacons" (1:1), one that had made his joy complete again and again.

Endnotes

Introduction

1 Chrysostom, Homily on Philippians, 2.1.1-2 in Mark J. Edwards, Ancient Christian Commentary on Scripture, New Testament VIII, Galatians, Ephesians, Philippians (Downers Grove, IL: InterVarsity Press, 1999), 208.

2 I want to acknowledge that I made use of ChatGPT to generate the first draft of the questions, but modified them to comply with the specific purpose of this study.

Chapter 1

3 Ambrosiaster, Epistle to the Philippians 1.1.1 in Mark J. Edwards, Ancient Christian Commentary on Scripture, New Testament VIII, Galatians, Ephesians, Philippians (Downers Grove, IL: InterVarsity Press, 1999), 207.

4 Ephesians, Philippians, and Colossians are grouped as the Prison Epistles. Philemon too is thought to have been written around the same time.

5 Lynn H. Cohick, Philippians (Grand Rapids: Zondervan Publishing House, 2013), 139.

6 This is based on the English Standard Version. Due to differences in the Greek text used, the King James Version has slightly more references.

7 James W. Thompson and Bruce W. Longenecker, Paideia Commentaries on the New Testament: Philippians and Philemon (Grand Rapids: Baker Academic Publishers, 2019), 5.

8 Thompson and Longenecker, Paideia, 4.

9 N.T. Wright, Philippians (Downers Grove, IL: InterVarsity Press, 2009), Kindle edition, loc. 18.

10 Andrew M. Selby, "Bishops, Elders, and Deacons in the Philippian Church: Evidence for Plurality from Paul to Polycarp," Perspectives in Religious Studies, Journal of the NABPR, 79-94.

11 Some do not identify the Seven as deacons since later in the

book of Acts, Philip is identified as "one of the Seven" (Acts 21:8) and not a deacon.

12 Joseph H. Hellerman, Philippians, Exegetical Guide to the Greek New Testament (Nashville, TN: Broadman and Holman, 2015), 10-11.

13 Gordon D. Fee, IVP New Testament Commentary, Philippians (Downers Grove, IL: InterVarsity Press, 1999), 67 (emphasis added).

14 Polycarp, To the Philippians 6.1; 11.1

15 James Moulton and George Milligan, The Vocabulary of the Greek Testament (Grand Rapids, MI: Eerdmans Publishing, 1963), 244.

Chapter 2

16 Edwards, Ancient Christian Commentary on Scripture, 209.

17 Barclay, Letters to the Philippians, Colossians, and Thessalonians, 13-15.

18 Tony Merida and Francis Chan, Exalting Jesus in Philippians (Nashville: Holman Reference, 2016), 24.

19 Augustine, On Grace and Free Will, 32, in Edwards, Ancient Christian Commentary on Scripture, 210.

20 Barclay, Letters to the Philippians, Colossians, and Thessalonians, 16.

21 J. A. Motyer, The Bible Speaks Today: The Message of Philippians (Downers Grove, IL: Intervarsity Press, 1984), 40-41.

22 See commentary on adelphoi ("brothers") in Philippians 1:12 in the NET Bible (Nashville: Thomas Nelson, 2019), 2245.

23 J. Scott Duvall and Verlyn D. Verbrugge, eds. Devotions on the Greek New Testament (Grand Rapids: Zondervan Publishing House, 2012), 90.

24 Bruce Metzger, A Textual Commentary on the Greek New Testament (Minneapolis: Fortress Press, 2008), 611-612.

25 Edwards, Ancient Christian Commentary on Scripture, 213.

26 Fee, Philippians, 62.

27 Ibid., 58.

28 James Riley Estep, Jr. "Biblical Qualities of an Elder," Part 1, Christian Standard (October 2012): 52-54; "Biblical Qualities

of an Elder," Part 2, Christian Standard (November 2012): 59-60. Jim Estep, "Biblical Qualities of Elders," Answer His Call (Joplin, MO: College Press, 2009), 47-58, 60.

Chapter 3

29 Barclay, Letters to the Philippians, Colossians, and Thessalonians, 25.
30 Ibid., 26.
31 Merida and Chan, Exalting Jesus in Philippians, 61.

Chapter 4

32 https://www.theodorerooseveltcenter.org/Learn-About-TR/TR-Encyclopedia/Culture-and-Society/Man-in-the-Arena.aspx (emphasis added).
33 Fee, Philippians, 75.
34 Ibid.
35 Cleon L. Rogers Jr. and Cleon L. Rogers III, The New Linguistic and Exegetical Key to Greek New Testament (Grand Rapids: Zondervan Publishing, 1998), 451.
36 Fritz Rienecker, Linguistic Key to the Greek New Testament (Grand Rapids: Zondervan Publishing House, 1982), 549.
37 Merida and Chan, Exalting Jesus in Philippians, 93.
38 Mark E. Hargrove, "The Christ Hymn as a Song for Leaders," Journal of Biblical Perspective in Leadership, 2(1): 19-31.
39 Donald Dawe, The Form of a Servant (Eugene, OR: Wipf & Stock, 2011).
40 Steven D. Cone, Theology from the Great Tradition (Edinburgh, Scotland: T & T Clark, 2017), 376-379.
41 Cyril of Alexandria, "Festival Letter," 10.4 in Edwards, Ancient Christian Commentary on Scripture, 238.
42 Rogers and Rogers, The New Linguistic and Exegetical Key to Greek New Testament, 452.
43 Hellerman, Philippians, 135.
44 Thomas Moore, Big Greek Idea Series: An Exegetical Guide for Preaching and Teaching -- Philippians (Grand Rapids: Kregel Academic, 2019), 129.
45 Chrysostom, "Homily on Philippians," 9.2.15-16 in Edwards, Ancient Christian Commentary on Scripture, 247.

46 Fee, Philippians, 107-108, 110.

47 David Allen, "'Paul Donning Mosaic Garb?' The Use of Deuteronomy 32 in Philippians 2:12-18," European Journal of Theology, 26(2): 135.

48 Leighten Ford, Transforming Leadership (Downers Grove, IL: IVP, 1993), 121.

49 Cohick, Philippians, 118, 129.

50 Richard H. Swartley, Eldership in Action through Biblical Governance of the Church (Dubuque, IA: Emmaus College Press, 2005), 31.

51 Swartley, Eldership, 75.

Chapter 5

52 J. Andrew Doole, "Was Timothy in Prison with Paul?" New Testament Studies, 65(1): 59-77.

53 Edwards, Ancient Christian Commentary on Scripture, 250.

54 Jim Estep, David Roadcup, Gary Johnson, What's Next? How Thinking Forward Moves the Church Forward. (Indianapolis, IN: e2 effective elders 2017), 84-98; James R. Estep Jr., "Transforming Groups into Teams," Management Essentials for Christian Ministries, Michael J. Anthony and James R. Estep, Jr. eds. (Nashville, TN: Broadman-Holman Publishers, 2005), 333-348.

55 While this quotation is widely attributed to President Reagan, there is no specific source or citation for it, but it does succinctly summarize his sentiments.

56 Fee, Philippians, 114.

Chapter 6

57 W. S. Campbell, "Judaizers," Dictionary of Paul and His Letters, Gerald F. Hawthorne, Ralph P. Martin, and Daniel G. Ried eds. (Downers Grove, IL: IVP, 1993), 512-516.

58 W. L. McCullough, "Dog," The Interpreter's Dictionary of the Bible, Volume 1 (Nashville: Abingdon Press, 1962), 862.

59 Ibid.

60 John C. Maxwell, The Maxwell Leadership Bible (Nashville: Thomas Nelson, 2018), 1421.

Chapter 7

61 I learned of this story from Dr. Mark Bailey, former President of Dallas Theological Seminary, when preaching on the passage in question. I later researched it online, and located a video of the race itself!

62 Rogers Jr. and Rogers III, 456.

63 NET Bible (Nashville: Thomas Nelson, 2019), 2249.

64 Reinecker, Linguistic Key, 559.

65 Jerome, "Dialog against the Pelagians," 1.15 in Edwards, Ancient Christian Commentary on Scripture, 260 [emphasis added].

66 Miroslav Balint-Feudvarski, "Sanctification through Knowledge and Imitation in Philippians," Kairos, 12(1): 23, 33-38.

67 Andrew D. Clarke, Serve the Community of the Church: Christians as Leaders and Ministers (Grand Rapids: Eerdmans Publishing, 2000), 193-194.

68 Clement of Alexandria, "Stromata," 3.14.95 in Edwards, Ancient Christian Commentary on Scripture, 264.

69 David R. Gray, "Christological Hymn: The Leadership Paradox of Philippians 2:5-11," Journal of Biblical Perspectives in Leadership, 2(1): 3-18.

Chapter 8

70 A. Katherine Brieb, "The One Who Called You . . . Vocation and Leadership in the Pauline Literature," Interpretation (April 2005): 158-159.

71 On a personal note, the author is a progressive dispensationalist, a form of premillennialism.

72 David Roadcup, "Elders who Disciple: One Key to an Effective Church," Christian Standard, September 1, 2021. Accessed September 14, 2024. https://christianstandard.com/2021/09/elders-who-disciple-one-key-to-an-effective-church/

73 Robert F. Hull Jr., "Constructing Euodia and Syntyche: Philippians 4:2-3 and the Informed Imagination," Priscilla Papers, 30(2): 6.

74 Edwards, Ancient Christian Commentary on Scripture, 266-267.

75 Frank Thielman, The NIV Application Commentary: Philippians (Grand Rapids: Zondervan Publishing, 1995, 227.

76 Vincent Michael Fiqueredo, "The Ancient Heart: What the Heart Meant to Our Ancestors," Journal of the American College of Cardiology, 78(9): 999.

77 James Riley Estep, Jr. and Brian Johnson, "The Apostle Paul's Concept of Education in the Church: Paul's Use of Paralambanō and Paradidōmi," Paper Presented at the North American Professors of Christian Education (Rochester, MN), 2005.

78 Jaramie Rinne, Church Elders: How to Shepherd God's People like Jesus (Wheaton, IL: Crossway, 2014), 66-67.

79 Wendy Cotter, "Woman's Authority Roles in Paul's Churches: Countercultural or Conventional?" Novum Testamentum, 36(4): 350-372.

80 Jim Estep, "Women as Deacons," DeaconStrong (Indianapolis, IN: e2 effective elders ministries, 2020), 31-44.

Chapter 9

81 Paraphrased from Tim Keller, The Prodigal God (New York: Penguin, 2011), 69-70.

82 Thompson and Longenecker, Paideia, 17. Note: The chart was amended to reflect the ESV translation used in this book but not in the original text.

83 Fee, Philippians, 185.

84 Chrysostom, Homily on Philippians, 15.4.9 in Edwards, Ancient Christian Commentary on Scripture, 270.

85 See Romans 15:26; 1 Corinthians 16:5, and 2 Corinthians 1:16, 2:13, 7:5, 8:1, 9:2-4; 11:9.

86 See 1 Thessalonians 2:2; Acts 17:1-7.

87 Cohick, Philippians, 195.

88 "Introduction to 1 Timothy," New International Study Bible (Grand Rapids: Zondervan Publishing House, 2020), 2126-2127.

www.ingramcontent.com/pod-product-compliance
Lightning Source LLC
Chambersburg PA
CBHW020204090426
42734CB00008B/934